God, Singleness, & Marriage

How the Bible gives purpose and
direction to singles

Unless marked otherwise, Scripture quotations are from *The Holy Bible, English Standard Version* ™, copyright © 2001 by Crossway Bibles, a publishing ministry of Good News Publishers. Emphasis has been added to some of the quotes.

Cover image: Adobe Stock. Cover design: Ben Khazraee.

Printed by CreateSpace

Thanks to Grace Church and my fellow pastors, Rod and Doug, for allowing me the time to think, pray, research, and write about this topic. I would also like to thank Charlie Greenwell, Tabitha Odediran, Blake Hudson, Derrik Nelson, my mom, Sandy, and my wife, Elisabeth, for the time and energy they spent reading and editing. I am also deeply indebted to many others whom I read and listened to as I composed this book. It is safe to say that none of the good ideas in this book are wholly mine.

Ben Khazraee
May 22, 2014
Thomasville, GA

Contents

Introduction   1

Section One: Singleness Redeemed-
How the Bible gives purpose and hope to singles

1. The Biblical Storyline and Singleness:
    How singleness is redeemed   7

2. A Biblical Vision for God-Glorifying Singleness:
    How singleness serves the Kingdom   25

3. The God of the Single (and Married):
    How a right view of God gives hope to us all   39

Section Two: Dangers of the Single Season-
Keeping watch on your soul

4. The Dangers of Discontentment, Envy, and Pride   51

5. The Dangers of Worldliness   63

6. The Dangers of Fear and Failing to Steward Time Well   75

Section Three: Living in the Single Season-
Honoring God as a single person

7. Honoring God by Maturing as a Christian Man or Woman   87

8. Honoring God as You Look for a Spouse   99

9. Finding a Good Thing:
    Biblical principles for finding a spouse   115

Conclusion:
A Wedding Reception That Will Change Our Lives   127

Introduction

Within the first two chapters and last four chapters of the Bible we find marriages (Gen. 2; Rev. 19). At the beginning of Jesus' earthly ministry we find him attending a wedding (John 2). Weddings and marriages seem to turn up at important moments in biblical history.

They are probably part of your experience, too. Maybe you have attended a few and the thought of weddings strikes a note of hope and joy as you look forward to your own marriage. Maybe you have attended many weddings and are tired of the recurring and painful question that inevitably comes during the reception: "So, when are you getting married?" For you, weddings bring up the painful fact that you may never be married. Or, it could be that you enjoy attending weddings but have little desire to get married.

The Most Important Thing about You

As we begin our journey to see what the Bible has to say about singleness and getting married, I want you to realize that the most important thing about you is not your marital status. It may feel that way at times. As many singles have noted, they feel like a single person in a married person's world. Every time you go out to eat and have to ask for "a table for one," you feel as if your most defining characteristic is the label "single."

However, the Bible makes it clear that the most important thing about you is that you are a Christian.[1] You are not a *single* Christian. You are a *Christian* who is unmarried. This is not semantics. I am trying to get at what the Bible says is the most defining reality for you, and it is not your marital status.

The Goal of This Book

That being said, your marital status does affect the way you live and experience life. And the Bible does say much about the topics of marriage, singleness, and relationships. My goal in the pages that follow is to bring some of the rich truths of the Bible on this issue to light.

If you are single and content, I hope that the words in this book will encourage and empower you for even greater fruitfulness and joy in serving the Lord. If you are single and hopeful of marrying in the near future, I hope that you will be encouraged to maximize your time as a single and to pursue

---

[1] Though maybe you are not a Christian. A Christian is not simply a person who goes to church or even likes Jesus. A Christian is a person who has recognized that they have sinned and rejected their Creator and are worthy of His just condemnation. They do not think they can earn God's forgiveness by doing good things. They understand that Jesus, God's perfect Son, lived the perfect life they failed to live and then died on the cross to satisfy the justice and wrath of God. They receive this blood-bought forgiveness by turning away from sin (repentance) and turning to Jesus as their only hope of salvation (faith). If you haven't done this, you should spend some time studying the gospel (good news) of God by reading the Gospel of Mark, from the Bible, with a Christian friend.

marriage in ways which glorify God. If you are single and struggling to be content, wondering if you have missed the opportunity to be married, I hope you will be encouraged to trust God and thrive under His care for you.

Where We Are Going

This book is divided into three main sections. The first is all about how the biblical storyline and the character of God give purpose and hope to singleness. It begins by tracing singleness through the Bible and demonstrating how God has redeemed the state of singleness for His glory and our good. The second chapter examines the most robust passage on singleness in the entire Bible, 1 Corinthians 7, in order to give you a vision for how to glorify God and utilize your singleness. The third chapter applies the doctrine of God to your understanding of singleness in order to strengthen your faith in God during an undesired time of singleness. Reader, you may be tempted to skip over this part. You might find it hard to read through these early chapters because you long for quick and practical steps to marriage. Let me encourage you to do the hard work of studying theology – only then will you find true hope and right practice.

The second major section of the book is about the dangers and temptations that seem most pronounced during the single season of life. All temptation is common to man, but we do well to examine what specific temptations Satan may use to lure us away from our devotion to Christ. Again, you may be tempted to skip this section, thinking that reading about sin is not encouraging. But remember that our enemy seeks to devour us (1 Pet. 5:8), and Jesus called us to watch and pray lest we enter into temptation (Matt. 26:41). You would not go to war with an enemy and ignore the specific points of vulnerability that he might seek to exploit against you. Neither should we expect to live the Christian life in this fallen world without examining our own weak points and shoring up our defenses.

The final major section gets into the practical aspects of living in the single season of life. The first chapter addresses issues that apply to *all* Christians while the last two look more specifically to Christians who are single but desire to be married. However, I do think that those who are not seeking marriage will still find these chapters beneficial.

We will conclude with a chapter about a wedding reception that all Christians will attend, which will be the most joyful wedding feast ever. Maybe you hate going to wedding receptions and being reminded that you lack what you so badly want. But I guarantee that this is one reception you will be glad to go to. We have a lot of pages to cover before we get there. So, get to reading.

Section One:
Singleness Redeemed

How the Bible gives purpose
and hope to singles

1

The Biblical Storyline and Singleness:

How Singleness is Redeemed

Have you ever read Genesis 2:18 and 1 Corinthians 7 back-to-back?

> Then the LORD God said, "It is not good that the man should be alone; I will make him a helper fit for him" (Gen. 2:18).

> To the unmarried and the widows I say that it is good for them to remain single as I am... So then he who marries his betrothed does well, and he who refrains from marriage will do even better (1 Cor. 7:8, 38).

Does this seem to contradict? At the beginning of the storyline, we read God saying "it is not good that man be alone" and then instituting marriage. But, by the time we get to the New Testament, we see Paul saying[2] that remaining

---

[2] Throughout this book I will refer to "Paul" saying or writing things, but I want to be sure you understand that God is the divine author of all Scripture who worked through human authors (2 Tim. 3:16).

unmarried is good and, in some circumstances, "better" than marriage. It seems that as the biblical storyline progresses, singleness goes from being "not good" to "good." How are we to make sense of this?

In the next two chapters, I want to spend some time trying to answer this question. In this chapter, we look at the big picture of the Bible and how marriage and singleness fit in to the storyline of the Bible. We will examine why singleness was an unwelcomed experience in the Old Testament and how it became a potentially good status for New Testament believers. In the next chapter, we will zoom in on 1 Corinthians 7 to catch the biblical vision for how singleness should serve the glory of God.

There is much at stake in understanding what the Bible has to say about singleness. A wrong view will result in singleness being wasted or marriage being idolized. A correct view will help you get a better grasp on the significance of both marriage and singleness in God's plan for the universe. I pray this will help you better understand your own place in God's plan.

The Big Picture of the Bible and Singleness

As we begin, it is important to understand that the Bible isn't a compilation of wise sayings, wonderful poems, and detailed laws. It does include all those things, but the Bible is actually a unified story about God and His dealings with His creation. Like any good story, the plot continues to develop with each passing page and, in the Bible's case, with each century of history.

As God's plans and promises unfold, we find that marriage and singleness *both* end up serving the Kingdom of God in unique ways. That is not, however, where the story starts. It begins with a focus on marriage and the offspring which marriage produces. How, then, do we get to a point where marriage *and* singleness serve the Kingdom?

I'll give you the reader's digest version here and the full version in the rest of this chapter.

1. In the Old Testament, the promise of offspring (or "seed") is central to the unfolding plan of redemption.[3] In the New Testament, the fulfillment of this promise comes *in Jesus Christ*.

2. In the Old Testament, believers personally experienced the blessings of God most tangibly and directly through marriage and the offspring it produced. In the New Testament, every believer experiences spiritual blessing *in Jesus Christ*.

. These two points provide the explanation for how and why things change over the course of biblical history. As you will note, the explanation has to do with the fact that God's plan to save a people for himself was designed to unfold over the

---

[3] By "redemption" I refer to God's plan to save a people for Himself. This salvation is from 1) God's own wrath against their sin, 2) from their bondage to Satan and sin, and 3) their spiritual deadness to the things of God.

span of time and covenants.[4] I will trace these two points through the Old, and then into the New Testament.[5]

The Old Testament: Marriage and Offspring are Good, but Singleness is Not

The Promised Seed and God's Plan of Redemption

Early in the biblical narrative God says he will make for Adam a helper compatible to him, namely woman (Gen. 2:15). Marriage is God's design, and it is intended to provide companionship and the ability to "be fruitful and multiply" as man and woman fulfill their God-given role of ruling the Earth (Gen 1:28, 2:18). This first couple becomes the parents of the entire human race.

God made Adam and Eve holy and happy, but things quickly go downhill. In Genesis 3, Adam and Eve are tempted by Satan and rebel against God. In the aftermath of this sin, God pronounces curses on all the parties involved. Physical and spiritual death is the consequence of sin. There is now a need to be saved from God's just wrath against sin.

However, God gives a ray of sunlight in the gloom of judgment. While cursing the serpent, who is Satan (cf.

---

[4] The Old Testament deals primarily with the Old Covenant that God made with the nation Israel. The New Testament is an account of the New Covenant that brings about the fulfillment of the Old, through Jesus Christ. My assumption is you are familiar with the basic storyline of the Bible. If not, you may want to check out the book by Mark Dever entitled, *What Does God Want of Us Anyway: A quick overview of the whole Bible.*

[5] I am indebted to Barry Danylak's book *Redeeming Singleness: How the storyline of Scripture affirms the single life* (Wheaton, IL: Crossway, 2010) for shaping much of my thinking in this area.

Revelation 12:9), God states that the offspring, or seed of the woman, will one day crush Satan's head (Gen. 3:15). *This is the first glimpse into God's plan to redeem a people from sin and Satan, and it involves the idea of offspring and, by extension, marriage.*

From Genesis 3:15 through the rest of the Old Testament, God's people await the promised seed of the woman who will come and defeat the ancient foe. This reality of a promised seed adds a new, redemptive urgency to the earlier command for man and woman to "be fruitful and multiply" (Gen. 1:28).

The Seed of the Woman Continues: The Abrahamic Covenant

When we get to Genesis 12, we find that the line of the promised seed zooms in on a man named Abram. God makes some pretty big promises to Abram, declaring,

> And I will make of you a great nation, and I will bless you and make your name great, so that you will be a blessing. [3] I will bless those who bless you, and him who dishonors you I will curse, and in you all the families of the earth shall be blessed (Gen. 12:2-3).

God promises to make Abram a great nation, a great name, and a blessing to all the families of the earth. It becomes clear *that offspring are central to God's promises to Abram, and to the world,* when we see God saying things like:

> Behold, my covenant is with you, and you shall be the **father of a multitude of nations.** No longer shall your name be called Abram, but your name shall be Abraham, for I have made you the **father of a multitude of nations**.

I will make you *exceedingly fruitful*, and *I will make you into nations*, and kings shall come from you. And I will establish my covenant between me and you and *your offspring* after you throughout their generations for an everlasting covenant, to be God to you and to *your offspring* after you (Gen. 17:4-7).

As you continue reading through Genesis, you will find that marriage and the offspring it could produce play a major role in the storyline and the anticipated fulfillment of God's promises.[6]

Personally Experiencing God's Blessings in the Old Testament: The Mosaic Covenant

Fast forwarding to Moses, we find that God's people, now the nation Israel, are living in Egypt. While the people are in Egypt, they are blessed with many offspring (Ex. 1:7), but they are not in the land God promised them. In fact, they are enslaved under Pharaoh. So, God acts to redeem His people from Egypt.

After rescuing His people from exile, God gives them His law. This is what is referred to as the Old Covenant. The law does not supersede the promises God made in Gen. 3:15 or to Abraham (See Galatians 3:16-18). "Why then the law? It was added because of transgressions, until the offspring should

---

[6] See Danylak *Redeeming Singleness*, pg. 49-52 where he deals with Genesis 26:2-5, 24; 28:13-15; 35:10-12. An important side note about these promises is that God himself must act to bring about His promises. Many of the women central to redemptive history are barren for long periods of time before God finally opens their womb. God shows that He is sovereign thus eliminating any room for human boasting (see Sarah [Gen. 11:30, 16:1, 17:15-16, 21:1-7], Rebekah [Gen. 25:21], Rachel [Gen. 29:31]).

come to whom the promise had been made" (Gal. 3:19a). That is, the law comes to reveal the people's sinfulness in clear and specific ways so that they will see their need for God's salvation in the "offspring" who is Jesus (cf. Romans 3:20). However, at this point in the storyline, the offspring has not yet come.

In the law, God promises blessings when the people obey. These blessings include physical offspring (Deut. 28:11). God also promises curses for disobedience. One of the curses for high-handed disobedience was that God would blot out a person's name (Deut. 29:18-20). If your name didn't continue (i.e., if your offspring didn't live on) you would be erased from the tangible experience of God's blessings. Barry Danylak summarizes it like this:

> Having one's name 'blotted out' (e.g., Deut. 29:20) was the capstone of personal disasters. No surviving children in ancient Israel meant the loss of one's inheritance, name, and covenantal blessings. Conversely, marriage and offspring were fundamentally necessary for the reception of all the covenantal blessings.[7]

So, in the Mosaic (i.e., Old) Covenant, we see that believers personally experienced the blessings of God in a tangible way through offspring. Legitimate offspring, of course, required marriage.

---

[7] Danylak, pg 69. He goes on to say, "Given this fact, it is not surprising to find within the Torah codified provisions to mitigate the likelihood of such a disaster occurring. One such provision was levirate marriage." Levirate marriage was when an unmarried man was called on to marry his deceased brother's wife if they had no children. The idea was that he was to raise up at least one offspring to carry on his dead brother's name and inheritance.

The Seed of the Woman Continues: The Davidic Covenant

As we press on in the biblical story, we come to King David, another significant person in the progression of God's plan of redemption. In 2 Samuel 7, God makes some big promises (another covenant) to David and his offspring.

If you compare this covenant to the promises made to Abraham in Genesis, it becomes clear that the line of promise is continuing through David. God promises to make David a great name (2 Sam. 7:9), to raise up his offspring (v. 12), and to establish his kingdom forever (v. 12-13).[8] Thus, the line of promise has zeroed in on David and his son.[9] What is new is that this long awaited offspring will not only be a Savior, but also the King of God's people. It becomes obvious, however, that David's immediate son, Solomon, will not be *the ultimate* kingly seed. At this point, God's people are still waiting for *the* promised offspring.

What We Have Seen so Far

Marriage, and the offspring it could produce, has been central in the overarching story of God's plan to redeem people. The people are awaiting the promised seed. Marriage and offspring have also been central in the everyday lives of individual Israelites because it was through these that they experienced many of the covenant blessings in tangible ways.

---

[8] Cf. Genesis 12:2 (name great and great nation), 13:16 (offspring), and 13:15 (land).

[9] 2 Sam 7:12-14a "When your days are fulfilled and you lie down with your fathers, I will raise up your offspring after you, who shall come from your body, and I will establish his kingdom. He shall build a house for my name, and I will establish the throne of his kingdom forever. I will be to him a father, and he shall be to me a son."

This explains why marriage was considered a necessity for every person in the Old Testament. And this is why those who were single or barren were not envied. In fact, they were pitied by others and often experienced great sadness.[10]

Something New is Coming: The Prophets

When we get to the prophets, however, we begin to see that a change is coming. God unveils more details about the One who will come to redeem His people. And, in the process, He has some pretty amazing things to say about the barren and unmarried.

For starters, in Isaiah 54:1, we read,

> "Sing, O barren one, who did not bear;
>> break forth into singing and cry aloud,
>> you who have not been in labor!
> For the children of the desolate one will be more
>> than the children of her who is married," says the LORD.

In light of what we have seen so far in the storyline, this is an astonishing call to singing. The one who is barren, without offspring, is called to sing. In this passage, God is referring to Israel as a barren one. She has broken the Mosaic Covenant and is experiencing the curses God promised.

But, the barren woman is to sing because her children will be "more than the children of her who is married." This is not referring to having physical babies. Why do I say that? Because Paul makes it clear, in the New Testament, that this is the promise of *spiritual* children.

---

[10] See Sara in Gen 16:1-2, Rachel in Gen. 29:1, Hannah in 1 Samuel 1:5-7.

In contrasting the New Covenant with the Old, Paul quotes this Isaiah passage in Galatians 4:26-28 when he says,

> But the Jerusalem above is free, and she is our mother. For it is written,
>
> > "Rejoice, O barren one who does not bear;
> > break forth and cry aloud,
> > you who are not in labor!
> > For the children of the desolate one will be more
> > than those of the one who has a husband."
>
> Now you, brothers, like Isaac, are children of promise.

In other words, God makes the barren one fruitful by bringing forth many "children of promise" (i.e., *spiritual* children) into the family of God. This is why Paul tells these *Gentiles* (i.e., non-Jewish believers) that this prophecy is fulfilled in their being included as "children of the promise."[11] This is one vista of the coming changes.

In Isaiah 56, there is yet another glimpse of change and hope for those who are not married. There we read about "the eunuch." A eunuch is a man who is unable to have children. Usually it was a man who had been taken captive to serve in a king's court and was castrated so that he would have undivided attention to serve the king (i.e., he would have no family of his own).

---

[11] As the ESV Study Bible notes on Isaiah 54:1, "The old covenant people of God, who failed to bless the world, were like a barren woman. Under the new covenant, God's people become the mother of a growing family." On another note, this should also give great hope to those who are married but barren.

In the Old Testament, being a eunuch was not a good thing. It meant being kept out of the assembly of God (Deut. 23:1) and missing out on the blessings of physical descendants. But, in Isaiah, we see an amazing statement of coming joy for the eunuch:

> and let not the eunuch say,
>   "Behold, I am a dry tree."
> For thus says the LORD:
> "To the eunuchs who keep my Sabbaths,
>   who choose the things that please me
>   and hold fast my covenant,
> I will give in my house and within my walls
>   a monument and a name
>   better than sons and daughters;
> I will give them an everlasting name
>   that shall not be cut off. (Is. 56:3b-5)

This one who was considered a "dry tree" has reason to rejoice if he belongs to God. God will give him "a monument and a name *better than sons and daughters*" and "an *everlasting name* that shall not be cut off." This is incredible. This eunuch is unable to experience the physical blessings in the Old Testament, but when God's salvation comes in its fullness (Is. 56:1) he will experience blessings greater than he could imagine.

So, change is coming. *Blessings are on the horizon for "singles."* Yet we are left wondering *how* this change comes about. To see how, we must go back to earlier sections of Isaiah and pick up the thread of the coming seed and redemption.

In Isaiah 7:14, we read that "the virgin shall conceive and bear a son, and shall call his name Immanuel [which means God with us]." Even though Israel has been unfaithful, God will be faithful to his promises to Abraham. And the hope rests in this Divine Son. Furthermore, this Divine Son will also sit "on the throne of David" (Is. 9:7). But, how will this Son bring about the promised redemption?

The answer is found in Isaiah 53 where we read of the "suffering servant" who is crushed by the LORD as a guilt offering for the sins of God's people (v. 4-6, 10).[12] This servant suffers the wrath of God to redeem sinners. He is "cut off out of the land of the living" (Is. 53:8b). That means he dies with no offspring and under the curse of God's law. But, in verse 10 we see things take a turn. We read,

> when his soul [i.e., the servant] makes an offering for guilt, he shall see his offspring; he shall prolong his days; the will of the LORD shall prosper in his hand. (Is. 53:10b)

The servant lives even after his death! How else could he "see his offspring" and "prolong his days" *after* he is crushed by the LORD? He dies to deal with the sins of his people, yet he lives and creates a people for himself (i.e., "his offspring"). As Barry Danylak puts it,

> Whereas the servant dies as a cursed man without family or progeny, in his death he becomes exalted of God (Is. 52:13) and blessed with an abundance of spiritual

---

[12] This servant is the same one we were reading about in the early chapters of Isaiah. Compare Is 53:2 with 11:1-10 where the word "young plant" is synonymous with "shoot" and both verses use the term "root." It is clear that the servant of Isaiah 53 is the root from David's line.

offspring who visibly emerge through the results of the obedience of his sacrificial death.[13]

So, the joy for barren Israel and barren individuals comes after this servant has suffered, died, and risen to see *His* offspring.

The New Testament: Marriage and Singleness are Good

In case you are unsure who this servant is, the New Testament makes it clear that Jesus *is the servant and the child* we read about in Isaiah.[14] Jesus is the Seed of the woman who crushes Satan.[15] He is the son of Adam, Abraham, and David.[16] With his arrival, the fulfillment of God's promised redemption comes. Additionally, the floodgates of promised blessings for the barren and the eunuch break open.

A New Perspective on Singleness Arrives

The first hint of this deluge of blessings comes as Jesus discusses marriage and divorce in Matthew 19:1-12. Jesus makes a statement that we often gloss over. It is one which would have been utterly shocking to His original audience.

---

[13] Danylak, pg. 101.

[14] For starters, see 1 Pet. 2:24, 2 Cor. 5:21, Matt 26:63, Acts 8:32, Rom. 5:18-19.

[15] See Matt 4:1, Mark 3:23, Jn. 13:27, Rev. 20:10.

[16] See Luke 3:38, Matt. 1:1.

Remember, the Old Testament has had a heavy focus on marriage and childbearing. In this context, Jesus says,

> "Not everyone can receive this saying, but only those to whom it is given. For there are eunuchs who have been so from birth, and there are eunuchs who have been made eunuchs by men, and **there are eunuchs who have made themselves eunuchs for the sake of the kingdom of heaven. Let the one who is able to receive this receive it**" (Matt. 19:11-12).

He says there are three classes of "eunuch." Two of which we have seen before in the Old Testament: 1. Eunuchs who were born that way, and 2. Eunuchs who have been made that way by men. Now, with His coming, there are eunuchs who "have made themselves eunuchs for the sake of the kingdom of heaven." In other words, now that the Seed has come, there is actually a category of "singles" that choose to be single for the purpose of serving the Kingdom of God!

The New Covenant and Spiritual Offspring

Now that Jesus has come and died and rose from the dead, the plan of redemption has entered into a new phase -- offspring are no longer merely physical. At the end of the Gospels Jesus gives the command to seek spiritual offspring when he says, "Go therefore and make disciples of all nations" (Matt. 28:19a). *The barren and eunuch and all singles can now be fruitful by seeking to have spiritual children through evangelism and discipleship.* It is clear that Paul, a single man, did this. He said to the Corinthian believers, "I became your father in Christ Jesus through the gospel" (1 Cor. 4:15b).

The New Covenant and the Believer's Blessings

In addition, the New Covenant changes the way individual believers experience the blessings of God. Now physical progeny and inheritance are not central. The spiritual family of God takes priority over physical family. Our love for Jesus must outweigh any other relationship. Jesus said, "Whoever loves father or mother more than me is not worthy of me, and whoever loves son or daughter more than me is not worthy of me" (Matt. 10:37).[17] The new importance of singleness does not mean "being alone" is now good (cf. Gen. 2:15). It means that in Christ we have a new family and are not alone, even when we are unmarried.

The New Covenant means blessings are for all who will obey God's Word, even if they are barren. In Luke 11:27-28, we see Jesus teaching this.

> As he said these things, a woman in the crowd raised her voice and said to him, "Blessed is the womb that bore you, and the breasts at which you nursed!" But he said, "Blessed rather are those who hear the word of God and keep it!" (see also Mark 3:31-35)

"True blessing is not in having children and a family (even having perfect children like Jesus!), but rather in truly hearing the word of God and keeping it."[18] *Those who hear and respond to the gospel of Jesus Christ now have every spiritual blessing guaranteed for eternity (Eph. 1:3-14).*

---

[17] This does not mean, however, we are to ignore our families (cf. 1 Tim. 5:8).

[18] Danylak, pg. 169.

Those who are saved by the gospel have a heavenly inheritance. This was true for the Old Testament saints, too. The difference is that we who live after the New Covenant has taken effect have the Spirit indwelling us as the guarantee of our inheritance. So, even if we lack a spouse and children, we have an internal witness that the blessings of God are ours. This is what Paul says of Christians:

> In him you also, when you heard the word of truth, the gospel of your salvation, and believed in him, were sealed with the promised Holy Spirit, who is the guarantee of our inheritance until we acquire possession of it, to the praise of his glory (Eph. 1:13-14).

New Testament believers can clearly see our inheritance is secured in the gospel by the Holy Spirit.

Putting it All Together

We began by comparing Genesis 2:15 and 1 Corinthians 7:8 and 38. We asked how it was possible to understand these passages together. How is it that singleness goes from "not good" to "good?" Now we have seen the answer.

Jesus is the Promised Offspring that Brought about the Promised Redemption

For starters, the Seed of the woman and the Abrahamic and Davidic covenants find their fulfillment in Jesus. Jesus brings in the New Covenant, and there is something truly "new" about the New Covenant. In the Old, the redemptive storyline was all about promises being made and preparing the way for the fulfillment of God's promises through one nation. Now that the promised Offspring has arrived, the focus is on going to tell the good news to all the nations. This is why we go from the command "be fruitful and multiply" in the physical sense (Gen 1:28) to "go therefore and make disciples of all nations" (Matt. 28:19a).

Jesus Secures Spiritual Blessings for Believers

Under the Old Covenant, the blessings of God were most clearly *experienced* by physical means: having offspring and an inheritance in the Promised Land. In the New Covenant, the blessings of God are experienced in terms of spiritual family and offspring. In addition, every believer has an inheritance from God that they can see by faith: "having the eyes of your hearts enlightened, that you may know what is the hope to which he has called you, what are the riches of his glorious inheritance in the saints" (Eph. 1:18).

Therefore Marriage and Singleness Are Valuable

Perhaps, a word of "balance" is helpful here. This "fresh" awareness regarding singleness is not meant to say that marriage is done away with or unimportant. Jesus has a high view of marriage (Matt. 19:1-9), and Paul says it was designed to put the relationship of Jesus and His bride, the Church, on display (Eph. 5:31-32). So, it isn't that marriage is spiritualized away and of minor importance.

Instead, under the New Covenant, marriage and singleness *both* serve God's plan of redemption. Also, married and single believers *both* experience the fullness of the New Covenant blessings through Christ at this very moment. With the arrival of the Seed and the redemption He brings, singleness was also redeemed.

Dear brother or sister, do you see that singleness is not a hindrance to serving God or experiencing His blessings? If He has redeemed you then thank Him for the innumerable blessings that are yours in Christ this very moment. Spend time thinking about how you can serve His Kingdom with your singleness. The single life can and should be a rich and full way of life for some Christians. Jesus redeemed it.

2

A Biblical Vision for God Glorifying Singleness:

How singleness serves the Kingdom

So far we have seen how singleness fits into the biblical storyline, and we have begun to see that it takes on new significance when we get into the New Covenant. We have seen that singleness has been redeemed, but we have not examined the most crucial passage which explains the purpose of singleness in the New Testament.

In this chapter, we will look at 1 Corinthians 7. [19] We will examine the "gift" of singleness, the principle of living the life God assigned to you, and the purpose of singleness in the New Covenant. As we do this, we will see the amazing service and joy that singleness can bring into the Christian life. We will catch a biblical vision for what redeemed

---

[19] This will not be an exposition of 1 Corinthians 7. That is beyond the scope of this book. The goal is just to focus on some of what this chapter tells us about singleness.

singleness looks like. Let's start by examining the "gift" of singleness.

The "Gift" of Singleness (1 Cor. 7:7-8)

Have you ever "re-gifted?" You know, when you receive a gift that makes you say, "Really, you shouldn't have" in the most literal sense of the phrase. Be honest. Surely, you have received a sweater that was not really what you wanted (though I'm sure it came in handy for the annual, ugly sweater party). Did you eventually "re-gift" that to another person?

Paul seems to say that singleness is a gift in 1 Corinthians 7:7-8 when he writes, in the context of talking about marriage,

> I wish that all were as I myself am. But each has his own gift from God, one of one kind and one of another. To the unmarried and the widows I say that it is good for them to remain single as I am.

Paul is a single man who is whole-heartedly devoted to serving God (1 Cor. 7:8). And he wishes all could be like that, but he recognizes not all have the same gifting from God.[20]

If you are single, maybe your response to this is the same as when you receive an unwanted Christmas sweater. Perhaps you think, "Is there a gift receipt so I can return it or a way to

---

[20] It is clear this is not a command and that Paul is not slighting the value of marriage. I say that because he just finished talking about the goodness of sexuality in marriage (and only in marriage) in vv. 1-6.

re-gift this thing?" Or maybe the thought of singleness being a gift excites you. Either way, we need to understand what the gift of singleness is and what it is not.

Two Different Types of "Gifts": General Blessing and Spiritual Enablement

We use the word "gift" to mean at least two different things in Christian circles. Sometimes we mean a gracious blessing God gives us (see James 1:17). For example, we might say that our friend is a gift from God. In that statement, we recognize him or her as a blessing to us that God sovereignly placed in our lives. We didn't deserve it, and God gave it. We may also refer to our privileges as Christians, such as access to God's throne in prayer, as a gift. *In other words, this first usage of the term "gift" is a general blessing to us as individual believers which does not require a unique empowerment of the Spirit of God in our lives.*

At other times, however, we may mean a *spiritual* gifting (see 1 Cor. 12:4). For example, a person may have the gift of teaching God's Word in a way that is clear and powerful. *In this case we are referring to a spiritual ability, empowered by the Spirit, which is given explicitly for the good of the Body of Christ (see 1 Cor. 12:7).*

What Type of "Gift" is Singleness?

So, in what sense does Paul think of singleness as a "gift?" *In this context, I believe he refers to it as a spiritual empowerment from God (a spiritual gifting).* One reason I think this is the case is later in 1 Corinthians Paul gives a full treatment on the topic of spiritual gifts. So it fits the context of this letter.

The main reason I think this, however, is that Jesus seems to affirm that there is a special gifting (not a general blessing) when he says, "...there are eunuchs who have made themselves eunuchs for the sake of the kingdom of heaven. *Let the one who is able to receive this receive it*" (Matt. 19:12). In other words, not everyone has this unique, Spirit-empowered gift, but if the Spirit enables you to receive it you should.

This is not to say that every unmarried person has the spiritual gift Paul and Jesus refer to. It is not singleness *per se* that is the spiritual gift. Barry Danylak summarizes the gift well when he writes,

> The *charisma* [i.e., gift] of singleness is a Spirit-enabled freedom to serve the King and the kingdom wholeheartedly, without undue distraction for the longings of sexual intimacy, marriage, and family.[21]

So, the spiritual gift of singleness isn't merely being unmarried. It is a purposeful singleness *that is not unduly distracted by human longings for marriage*. Just to be clear, this does not mean these individuals have no longings for marriage. It simply means God empowers them to live without a *strong urge* (i.e., one that is often distracting) for marriage.[22] *The gifting of singleness is a divine enablement to*

---

[21] Danylak, pg. 200.

[22] I do not believe God necessarily gives you a spiritual gift and never replaces it with others. He gives gifts which are needed in carrying out his work. In other words, a person gifted with teaching isn't simply one who is humanly skilled in teaching. Instead, they have the Spirit of God empowering them. But, God, in his wisdom, may determine a different need and give a new gift to that person for the good of the body he is in. The same is true of singleness. If you sense the gifting of singleness, do not assume that God could never give you a spouse.

give undivided attention to serving the Lord. It is freedom from the distractions of a strong urge for physical family in order to benefit the family of God.

Therefore, the gift of singleness is not merely being unmarried in God's providence. You may find that you are unmarried but have a strong desire to be married. As Jesus pointed out, there are some who are eunuchs not by choice but because of circumstances (Matt. 19:12).

Even if this describes you, I believe your singleness is a gift from God. Let me say it again because it may have shocked you. God even intends times of singleness that you may not desire as a good gift. It is a gift in the first (general) sense described above. God gives His children the general blessing of trials. Not that suffering in itself is good but that what God intends and accomplishes through it is for our good (Rom. 8:28, 5:1-5). So, you may not have the spiritual gift of singleness, but you can and should joyfully receive it as a gift from your Father (James 1:2).

Whether or not you have the spiritual gift of singleness, Paul has an important principle for you about how to understand your current status of being unmarried.

The Principle: Live Where God Has You (1 Cor. 7:17-24)

When we come to verses 17-24, Paul digresses to give us a general principle. That principle, which comes in the context of Paul discussing marriage, applies to all Christians. It is succinctly stated at the beginning, middle, and end of this section of verses.

> Only let each person **lead the life that the Lord has assigned to him**, and **to which God has called him** (v. 17).

> Each one should **remain in the condition in which he was called**. (v. 20).

> So, brothers, **in whatever condition each was called, there let him remain** with God (v. 24).

In between these statements, Paul gives two illustrations of his point. The first refers to the issue of whether or not a person was circumcised before becoming a believer in Jesus (i.e., whether or not they were a Jew or Gentile at the time of their conversion). The second discusses those who become Christians but are slaves. In both cases, he is basically saying, "Your status does not affect your standing before God, so don't focus your whole life around trying to change those things."

The main point, therefore, is that God is sovereign over the circumstances of our lives. He graciously oversees each detail including our ethnicity, social standing, opportunities (and lack thereof), and, yes, our marital status. And, none of these circumstances will prohibit us from serving God or enjoying the fullness of His blessings.

He bought us with a price, and we are to serve Him no matter what our God given circumstance is in life (v. 23). We are to "lead the life" that the Lord assigns us (v. 17). God does not consider one condition or status as better than others in terms of our ability to serve Him. If this were true He would change our circumstances. To summarize, "Whether a Christian is married or single, circumcised or uncircumcised, slave or free, makes no difference to God…so there is no need to change."[23]

While a change of status is not necessary, and must not inhibit contented living before God, that does not mean that a change of status is prohibited. This is clear when Paul tells the slaves, "But if you can gain your freedom, avail yourself of the opportunity" (v. 20b). Paul makes this same point in other parts of this chapter when he says that it is not wrong to get married (v. 8-9, 28).

If you have a desire to get married, what implications does this have for you? First, you should not make your life revolve around finding a spouse. Instead, lead the life God has called you to at this moment. You ought to bloom where the Lord has planted you. Singleness does not prohibit or limit you from serving God.

Secondly, you should remain where you are "with God" (v. 24). Those last two words should bring great encouragement and exhortation for you. Be encouraged that you are not alone even if you are single. Be exhorted to make your focus in life on staying near God.

Reasons to Remain Single (1 Cor. 7:25-38)

Now we come to the most central passage about the purpose of singleness in the New Testament. Here Paul deals with the specific issue of those who currently are engaged or who are

---

[23] Ciampa, Roy and Brian Rosner, *The First Letter to the Corinthians,* In the Pillar NT Commentary Series, ed. DA Carson (Grand Rapids Michigin: Eerdmans Publishing Company, 2010), pg. 397.

considering seeking a spouse.[24] His advice is that they hold off on getting married. It is not a binding command as he makes clear when he says "But if you do marry, you have not sinned" (v. 28a, cf. v. 36). But he does give three reasons for advocating singleness.

Less Worldly Troubles (vv. 26-28)

Paul's first reason comes in the context of the present crisis that the Corinthians were facing.

> I think that *in view of the present distress it is good for a person to remain as he is.* Are you bound to a wife? Do not seek to be free. Are you free from a wife? Do not seek a wife. But if you do marry, you have not sinned, and if a betrothed woman marries, she has not sinned. *Yet those who marry will have worldly troubles, and I would spare you that* (1 Cor. 7:26-28).

Although we don't know what this distress was, it was severe enough to make them wonder if they should go through with marriage. If it was persecution, marriage provides a spouse you will fear losing to prison, torture or death. If it was food shortages, marriage, and the children it was likely to produce, would add to the difficulty. In any case, "those who marry will have worldly troubles" (v. 28b). So, Paul's first point is practical.

---

[24] The word translate "betrothed" in the ESV text is actually the Greek word for "virgins." Given the context (especially verse 36) the ESV translates it as "betrothed." Ciampa and Rosner think that Paul has in mind those who are betrothed and those wondering if they should seek a young woman to marry (Ibid., pg. 333).

How does this apply to us in our modern, Western culture? The basic principle means that "We need wisdom to discern the times and understand our circumstances so as to know the best way to glorify God and avoid putting ourselves or others under unnecessary duress." [25]

Perhaps it could apply to those considering going to a dangerous mission field in which having a spouse and children would bring added troubles. Outside of that, I do not think we, in the West, are currently experiencing distress of the same intensity as the Corinthians. There are economic and political woes, but none of these seem to be a good reason for us to put off marriage at the present time.

We must be careful not to allow the selfish desire of an easy life to be substituted for Paul's point here. A desire to achieve one's own goals or to knock a few items off of a "bucket list" before marriage is self-focus, not biblical wisdom. A preference for living alone in order to avoid conflict or to avoid serving another person is not what Paul has in mind by "less worldly troubles." The Christian life is all about dying to self in order to love God and others.

More Heavenly Minded (vv. 29-31)

The second reason for the encouragement to remain single is the fact that the time of this present Earth is relatively short.

> This is what I mean, brothers: the appointed time has grown very short. From now on, let those who have wives live as though they had none, and those who mourn as though they were not mourning, and those who rejoice as

---

25 Ibid., pg. 338.

though they were not rejoicing, and those who buy as though they had no goods, and those who deal with the world as though they had no dealings with it. *For the present form of this world is passing away* (1 Cor. 7:29-31).

Every believer since the time of Christ, has been living in the "last days." This is what Paul means when he says, "For the present form of this world is passing away" (v. 31). Since the end is coming, their perspective should be different than those who are oblivious to this fact. Paul tells them to live as though this world is not all there is -- because it is not. Their marital status, earthly sadness and joys, and material possessions are not the determining factors in how they live. Eternity is.[26]

So, what does this mean for us? We should not assume our joys, struggles, and marital status in this world are ultimate. Instead, we are to live like those who really believe Christ's kingdom is coming and that it is imminent. We must live with our hope and joy set on heaven and not the temporary things of this Earth. We are to live in this world, but we must have "a sober assessment of life's up and downs in the light of something of greater significance."[27] So, when it comes to our marital status, remaining unmarried is a good way to live in light of the coming Kingdom. Marriage isn't bad or wrong, but it should not be your ultimate goal in life.

---

[26] He does not say that they are "not married" or that they do not have joy and sorrow or that they do not participate in business transactions. He assumes all those things are true. The point, therefore, is not to live disconnected from reality but to live in light of ultimate reality such that it transforms your perspective on what matters most.

[27] Ibid., pg. 347.

Undivided Devotion to the Lord (vv. 32-35)

The third reason it is good to remain single is the freedom singleness brings for undivided devotion to the Lord. Unlike the previous two points, *I believe this reason actually gives the goal and vision for singleness as a Christian.* If you have the gift of singleness, this must be the reason and goal of your singleness. And, if you are single but desire marriage, this should be your perspective while you remain single lest you waste the trial God has given you. So what does Paul say?

> I want you to be free from anxieties. The unmarried man is anxious about the things of the Lord, how to please the Lord. But the married man is anxious about worldly things, how to please his wife, and his interests are divided. And the unmarried or betrothed woman is anxious about the things of the Lord, how to be holy in body and spirit. But the married woman is anxious about worldly things, how to please her husband. I say this for your own benefit, not to lay any restraint upon you, but to promote good order and to secure your undivided devotion to the Lord (1 Cor. 7:32b-35).

Paul's goal for singleness is "to secure your undivided devotion to the Lord" (v. 35b). Marriage necessitates time and energy being directed into one particular relationship. Singleness, on the other hand, provides immense freedom when it comes to time, energy, and opportunities.[28] As Dr. John MacArthur writes,

---

[28] I realize that this is not the case for those who are single parents. Your situation is a bit unique because you do have relationships which require marriage-like time and energy.

Marriage does not prevent great devotion to the Lord, and singleness does not guarantee it. But singleness has fewer hindrances and more advantages. It is easier for a single person to be singleminded in the things of the Lord. The married Christian has no choice. His interests must be divided. He cannot be faithful to the Lord if he is unfaithful to his family.[29]

So what does this mean for you? It means that you have a stewardship of extra time, energy, and resources to invest in broad service to the Kingdom of God. You have broader ministry potential.

If you are single, you may have more freedom with regard to *time*. There is not a spouse waiting on you or in need of your service, so, use your time to serve the saints in your church. Pour more time and energy into having and raising spiritual offspring (evangelism and discipleship). You may have more discretionary *money* because there are not additional mouths to feed and houses with more bedrooms to be purchased. So use your extra income to send missionaries and to give to your church. Perhaps you should even consider becoming a missionary.[30]

How Do You See Your Singleness?

The purpose of your singleness is to have undivided devotion towards God. Is that your perspective? The goal of singleness

---

[29] MacArthur, John, *1 Corinthians* In The MacArthur New Testament Commentary series (Chicago, IL: Moody Press, 1984), pg. 184.

[30] Though not every person who is single is called to be a missionary.

is not to allow more time to enjoy hunting or traveling or whatever hobby you enjoy. Singleness is not designed to make life all about *you,* rather it is intended to free you up to make life all about *Christ.* That is the biblical vision for singleness.

This is true whether you are in an undesired season of singleness or if you are exercising the spiritual gift of singleness. Either way you have a choice to make. Will you see your singleness as the God-glorifying opportunity it is meant to be or will you waste it? Will you turn your singleness into bondage by seeking your own personal ambitions or will you enjoy the freedom of undivided devotion to the Lord? If you desire marriage, will you spend inordinate amounts of the time and energy looking for a spouse or will you live as you were called while you trust God with your unmet desires? Your vision of singleness will determine if you waste it or if you are blessed in it. How do you see your singleness?

3

The God of the Single (and Married):

How a right view of God gives hope to us all

"You just have to trust God with your singleness." Perhaps you have heard that statement many times as a single man or woman. Maybe you think it is just a trite Christian expression and feel like it minimizes your pain. In one sense, you may be right. I don't know the motives of the people who have said that to you. And you may be tempted to interpret the suggestion of "just trust God" as one that makes it sound like your situation is hopeless. But, it is my prayer that you will see that trusting God with your whole life is the path to joy. It's not simply that you "just have to trust God," rather it is that you have the profound joy of trusting your faithful Father God.

Why Believing Right Doctrine Matters

God is who He is no matter what our present life situation may be. No matter what our marital status is, God is still

God. His attributes remain the same. His right to rule remains the same, and His trustworthiness remains the same, even though our trust might wane (2 Tim. 2:13). Many of us assent to these truths, but, if we are honest, we are tempted to disbelieve them when life isn't unfolding as we had envisioned.

This is precisely why it is important to spend some time, in a book on singleness, looking at who God is and examining our own hearts to uncover and battle against pockets of unbelief. If we are to glorify God and joyfully serve Him in singleness or marriage, we must see Him clearly and believe what we see. So, when I speak of God in this chapter, I will say many things that you might intellectually affirm. However, you may find that you have functionally forgotten some of these realities when it comes to your thoughts regarding your marital status. I want to bring the reality of who God is to bear on your current circumstances. Specifically, we will look at God's sovereignty, goodness, and wisdom as it relates to singleness.[31]

So, read this section carefully with a heart that humbly seeks to know and trust God more. In fact, maybe you should take a minute now to pray that God helps you to do that.

God is Sovereign

To say that God is sovereign means that He exercises supreme power and control at all times, in all situations, and over all things. I don't have space here to provide all the

---

[31] It would be good to spend time studying the attributes of God. I suggest *The Knowledge of the Holy* by Tozer or *The Attributes of God* by AW Pink.

biblical evidence for this, but the clear testimony of the Bible, from cover to cover, is that God supremely and powerfully rules over everything. [32] Nothing is outside of his control. *Nothing*! Not even evil and suffering. Lamentations 3:37-38 shows God's control over the whole spectrum of life:

> Who has spoken and it came to pass,
>   unless the Lord has commanded it?
> Is it not from the mouth of the Most High
>   that good and bad come?[33]

My guess is that if you have been a Christian for any length of time that you have come to believe this fact about God. However, I wonder if you have functionally failed to apply this truth to your relationship status. Perhaps it comes out in a thought that wonders if you are still single because you missed that last singles' event. I'm not suggesting we have no responsibility when it comes to finding a spouse; I am saying that God is sovereign over our current relationships *and* lack thereof.

Now, if we just ended our discussion of God here we would have a truncated understanding of Him. We would also probably fall into fatalism instead of trusting God. But, the Bible shows us that God's sovereignty is not the same as fatalism, because God is also good and wise in His exercise of His sovereignty.

---

[32] A good study on this topic is found in Jerry Bridges' book *Trusting God Even When Life Hurts.*

[33] While God is not to blame for evil, He, nonetheless, is sovereign over it. That is a good thing. If God were not in control then we would have no reason to believe His promises, for they might at any moment be overcome by Satan's evil plots. But, as we see in the first chapter of the book of Job, God rules even over Satan. As we see at the cross, God rules even over the greatest act of human evil, namely the crucifixion of the perfect Son of God (see Acts 2:23, which shows the guilt of the people and the sovereignty of God).

God is Good

By *good* I mean loving, kind, merciful, and gracious. God is not an autocratic ruler. He is the *Father* of those who belong to Him through Jesus Christ. And as a perfect Father, His heart is full of good things for His children. Jesus affirms this in Matthew 7:11 when He says,

> If you then, who are evil, know how to give good gifts to your children, how much more will your Father who is in heaven give good things to those who ask Him!

It is true that what a child *wants* is not always truly good at that moment. Just because a two- year old wants candy for dinner doesn't mean that a loving father will give it to him. But my suspicion is that you have an easier time believing that than you do believing that God is really as good as He says He is. So let's spend a minute looking at our temptation to doubt God's ubiquitous goodness.

The temptation to doubt God's goodness goes way back to a Snake in a garden who successfully convinced our first parents that God might not be as good as they initially thought.

The doubt surfaces again in Israel's history when God delivers them from their bondage in Egypt, and they quickly begin to wonder if God only freed them to let them die of hunger and thirst in the middle of nowhere (Ex. 16:2-3, 8).

Later in the biblical storyline, we see that old Serpent trying the same temptation on Jesus when he says, "If you are the Son of God, command these stones to become loaves of bread" (Matt. 4:3). [34] Jesus had been in the desert fasting for 40 days. Matthew tells us that the Spirit of God lead him out there (4:1). So, Satan is basically saying, "God is your Father isn't He? Has He led you out here and left you starve in this wasteland? That doesn't sound like a *good* Father. Perhaps you should take matters into your own hands." Thankfully, Jesus did not fail as Adam and Eve, Israel, or you and I have. He didn't listen to the lies of Satan or prefer His belly over God.

Brothers and sisters, don't fall for this questioning of God's goodness. Don't judge God's goodness based on your timetable and your cravings. Instead, trust His goodness based on the greatest demonstration of mercy ever: the sacrificing of His Son in your place so that He might offer you His eternal joy by forgiving your sin. Romans 8:32 says, "[God] who did not spare his own Son but gave him up for us all, how will he not also with him graciously give us all things?" He gave us the best gift! How could we doubt that He has kind intentions toward us? To quote pastor CJ Mahaney,

> Your greatest need is not a spouse. Your greatest need is
> to be delivered from the wrath of God- and that has
> already been accomplished for you through the death and
> resurrection of Christ. So why doubt that God will provide

---

[34] The reason I say "the same temptation" is because Jesus is, in the temptation narrative, reliving Israel's wilderness wanderings. The difference is that where they failed to trust the Father, Jesus succeeded!

a much, much lesser need? Trust His sovereignty, trust His wisdom, trust His love."[35]

Look to the cross as the ultimate display of God's goodness to you, and then trust that He is a good Father in every area of your life. God was not stingy in showing us His saving grace and goodness. Surely He will not be stingy in doing good to us all the days of our lives (Psalm 23:5-6). He doesn't give His children stones to eat. You may hunger for the intimacy you think a spouse would bring, but do not allow this desire to cloud your judgment of who God is. He has given you Himself in Jesus Christ. He has not withheld the best gift in the universe, so do not doubt his goodness.

Now, if we stop here we have not gone far enough. If God were simply sovereign and good, He may *desire* to do what is best and *be able* to do what is best, but He may not *know* the best way to achieve His good purposes. Thus, we would still find it hard to trust Him in a trying time of singleness. So, let's look at God's wisdom.

God is Wise

As theologian Wayne Grudem puts it, *"God's wisdom means that God always chooses the best goals and the best means to those goals."*[36] This is the consistent testimony of the Bible (see Rom. 16:27, Job 9:4, Ps. 104:24).

---

[35] Quoted by Joshua Harris in *Boy Meets Girl* (Sisters, Ore.: Multnomah, 2000), p. 213.

[36] Grudem, W. A. *Systematic Theology: An introduction to biblical doctrine* (Grand Rapids, MI: Inter-Varsity Press, 1994), pg. 193.

This, too, is an area where our functional theology may differ from our stated theology. In a long season of singleness, we are often tempted to think our plans are wiser than God's. We might not say that, but we reveal it as we complain and grumble when His wisdom doesn't match ours.

In God's wisdom, all things work together for the good of those who love Him (Rom. 8:28). Everything! Even an undesired season of singleness or the loss of a spouse through death or an unwanted divorce works for the good of those who love God. Those *things* may not all be good in and of themselves, but in God's wisdom they are the best means to accomplish the best ends. The "good" ends are defined as God conforming us to the image of Jesus (Rom. 8:29). So, even our trials, because they serve to make us more like Christ, are wisely ordained by our Father.

This doesn't mean we can never cry out to God in a trial with the words of the Psalmist, "How long, O Lord?" (Ps. 13:1). But it does mean we must not question His wisdom as if we *know* better. The Psalmist had honest questions that caused him to run to God. However, we, at times, hide behind questions which simply veil our bitterness and distrust of God. So, while we must run to God with questions, we must not turn those questions into accusations that we know how to run God's world, and our own lives, better than He does.

When we really believe God is wise, we will find great encouragement. To quote Grudem again,

> Every day of our lives, we may quiet our discouragement
> with the comfort that comes from the knowledge of
> God's infinite wisdom: if we are his children, we can know

that he is working wisely in our lives, even today, to bring
us into greater conformity into the image of Christ.[37]

You might be thinking, "Yes, I want to be conformed to the
image of Christ, but marriage would provide even more
opportunities for that. Living with a fellow sinner would
challenge my selfishness more." It is true that living with a
fellow sinner helps us see more of our selfishness. But the
point is that God has not lost sight of the best means by
which He will conform you to the image of Christ. For now,
that is in a season of singleness. Besides, if you are living in
true, biblical community, you will have plenty of
opportunities to see your selfishness challenged by your
brothers and sisters in Christ.

We must not question God's wisdom as if we know what is
best for ourselves. After all, do we see the beginning from
the end? Do we know all things? Are we really in a position
to know what is best? Only God is in such a position (Job 38-
39).

If This is True, Then He is Trustworthy

I hope you see how important theology is. Not just what we
say we believe but what we actually cling to and functionally
believe. This is not a "grin and bear it" theology. This is
"trust His heart when you can't trace His hand" theology.
Jerry Bridges put it well when he said,

> Trusting God in the midst of our pain and heartache
> means that we accept it from Him. There is a vast

---

[37] Ibid., pg. 194.

difference between acceptance and either resignation or submission. We can resign ourselves to a difficult situation, simply because we see no other alternative. Many people do that all the time. Or we can submit to the sovereignty of God in our circumstances with a certain amount of reluctance. But to truly accept our pain and heartache has the connotation of willingness. An attitude of acceptance says that we trust God, that he loves us, and knows what is best for us.[38]

So, what is your functional trust in God? Take some time to examine where your stated beliefs about God fail to match your actual (lived-out) beliefs. When you are tempted to question His sovereignty, goodness, or wisdom, turn your thoughts to Scripture, which affirms those very things. Stop listening to yourself and start talking to yourself. Stop letting your mind run wild with thoughts which question God's sovereignty, goodness, and wisdom, and, instead, remind yourself of what is actually true from Scripture.

If you are honest with yourself, I believe you will see some pockets of unbelief. I know that is true as I look at my life. When you see these areas, confess the sin to the Lord and thank Him that Jesus perfectly trusted the Father for you! His righteousness counts for you. Then, ask God to give you the grace to trust Him more and more.

Your whole Christian life is one of trusting in the sovereign, good, and wise Father. The season of singleness, whether it is short or a lifetime, is no exception. This is not a cliché when

---

[38] Bridges, Jerry, *Trusting God,* (Colorado Springs, Colo.: NavPress, 1988), p. 102.

I say, "Trust God and put all your hope in Him." Sometimes people say, "Trust God" because they just don't know what else to say or because it sounds spiritual. In this context, however, I believe we have developed a good foundation to say, "Trust God."

Section Two:
Dangers of the Single Season

Keeping watch on your soul

4

The Dangers of Discontentment, Envy, and Pride

Changes in seasons bring many blessings. We can see the beauty of autumn leaves, feel the invigorating splash of cold air in the winter, enjoy the vibrant foliage of the spring, and bask in the radiant sun of summer. However, changes in seasons also can bring season-specific difficulties. In some places, summer brings dangerous drought or flooding. In other places spring brings violent storms. Each season carries unique blessings and dangers.

The same is true in the seasons of life. Times of old age and young age each have blessings and trials. The same is true of marriage and singleness. In this section, we will spend some time thinking about a few common temptations faced in the single season of life.

Before diving in, let me give three quick caveats.

First, these temptations and sins are not unique to those who are single. All temptation is common to all kinds of people. The goal here is to look at a few areas of temptation which tend to be prevalent in a season of singleness.

This brings me to the next caveat; don't think I am insinuating that because you are single you must be struggling with all these temptations or that you fit every example I give. I am simply offering some thoughts and praying God will help you evaluate your own heart on these matters. Since we all tend to have skewed views of ourselves, it may be good to have a trusted Christian friend help you in this analysis of yourself.

The third caveat is that the single season may be a permanent season. This is where the analogy of seasons breaks down. God, in His wise and good plan, may not give you a season of marriage. I say this because I don't want to give you false, unbiblical expectations. I don't want you to think, "If I am just really good God will give me what I want." The point is to look at potential dangers and to seek to honor God by avoiding sin and putting on righteousness.

With these caveats in mind, let's ask God to do His sanctifying work in our lives as we look to His Word.

Discontentment

The first major temptation is that of discontentment. This is not unique to those who are unmarried, but it is often a temptation when a person seriously desires a good gift which God has not yet given. Discontentment arises when we fail to trust God with our desires and, instead, place our hope in changed circumstances. It becomes a more pronounced temptation the longer the undesirable circumstances continue. For example, you might have a good desire to be married. Discontentment enters when you start thinking "I *must* be married if I am to be happy." And the longer your relationship status is "unmarried," the more unhappy and ungrateful you become.

Discontentment usually manifests itself in a heart that complains, either directly or indirectly, against God when desires are not met. It is often accompanied by ungratefulness for the good gifts and sustaining grace God has given. This is deadly to the soul if left unchecked, for it involves a heart that is not totally satisfied in God and His provision.

Additionally, discontentment provides a poor testimony to those watching your life. As Andreas Kostenberger and David Jones write,

> When singles display habitual discontentment with their present marital status, they communicate to a watching world that Jesus is insufficient for them or that perhaps he is incapable of meeting their desires.[39]

Before discussing how to resist the temptation towards discontentment, let me mention two things that are quite *unhelpful*. The first is *coping*. Coping is survival mode. It is seeing yourself as a victim, rather than as having a stewardship from God. It is just trying to get along until God finally brings you that special someone.

The person who is coping may try to pack his or her schedule so full that there isn't ever time to think about a desire for relationship. And maybe this is even mistaken for contentment, but contentment is not merely survival. It is not dulling the pain until the relief of marriage comes. True

---

[39]*God Marriage and Family*, (Wheaton, IL: Crossway Books, 2004), pg. 197.

contentment is not coping. It is thriving under the providence of God, even the hard providence of God. It is actively using the time and energy you have as a single person for "undivided devotion to the Lord" (1 Cor. 7:35).

The second unhelpful thing is *fantasy*. You may constantly imagine how great life would be "if only I were married." Or you may regularly drift off into thoughts about that ideal man or woman. Perhaps you read novels (even "Christian" ones) or watch movies and shows which feed this type of thinking.

Let me encourage you to put this thinking, and the things which feed it, aside (Phil. 4:6-8). You may think you are being content because you are not throwing yourself at every eligible bachelor or bachelorette that darkens the door of the church, but this is not the same as contentment. The "if only" thoughts will quickly lead to discontentment, and they will not stop after you say "I do." Once you are married you will dream about a million other things: having children, a day when your children are not so needy, having time and money for vacations, retiring, being young again, etc. As Clint Archer wrote:

> There is a lie that many people believe: that to be happy their circumstances need to change. If they are sad and single, they believe they will be happy when the nuptials are said. But you are the same person you were walking up the aisle as you are walking down it. If you are a discontent person, then you will soon transfer your

discontent to your spouse. Discontent with a spouse
quickly degenerates into malcontent. Then bitterness.[40]

You might be thinking, "But marriage is a good gift. It is not wrong to desire it." To which I say, it is a good gift, but good gifts make terrible gods. Gifts are never intended to be where we find our ultimate satisfaction. When we start looking to created things to do what only God can do – namely satisfy our deepest longings and provide lasting joy – we will *always* be discontent.

Don't let marriage become an idol in your life. If you are willing to sin to get it, or sin if you don't get it (with discontentment for example), it has become an idol. That may seem like a big claim, but consider that if we are willing to sin against God in pursuit of something or someone else, then that thing or person is, at that moment, more important to us than God.

So what is the solution to discontentment? The greatest cure to discontentment is reflecting on the goodness and wisdom of God. When you are tempted to be discontent, ask yourself if you really believe God is good and wise in withholding the gift of marriage from you at this moment. If you are given to discontentment, I think you will find that, at least functionally, you have some doubts about one or both of these truths. Or, perhaps, you have begun to value God's gifts more than you value God himself.

The good news is that contentment is something which we can learn. Paul said,

[40] "Why Isn't a Pretty Girl Like You Married? Staying Stag Pt. 2." Accessed at thecripplegate.com on June 15, 2013.

> I have *learned* in whatever situation I am to be content. I know how to be brought low, and I know how to abound. In any and every circumstance, I have learned the secret of facing plenty and hunger, abundance and need (Phil. 4:11b-12).

Then he tells us what the secret to contentment is: "I can do all things through him who strengthens me" (v. 13). In Christ, he had all he needed to faithfully serve God and others. Thank God that He gives us the strength to be content, and in that strength, work on putting on contentment.

And what is contentment? As Robert Jones puts it,

> It is having a satisfied mind in any situation. It is finding inner satisfaction in God alone and in His provisions for you...It is consciously enjoying the fact that God is good, even when your circumstances are not.[41]

Does all this mean you should not pray for God to provide a spouse? Not at all! God tells his children to come to Him with requests for His good gifts. What it does mean, however, is that we should pray with a satisfaction in all that God is, no matter what He gives.

Envy

Envy is very closely tied to discontentment. The heart that is not happy in God in tough circumstances will be prone to be

---

[41]"Learning Contentment in All Your Circumstances," Journal of Biblical Counseling, Fall 2002, pg. 53.

jealous of others who it perceives have the coveted blessings. As Jerry Bridges describes it,

> *Envy* is the painful and oftentimes resentful awareness of an advantage enjoyed by someone else. Sometimes we want the same advantage, leading to the further sin of covetousness. And sometimes we just resent the other person having something we don't have.[42]

Such envy is often expressed in a disdain for those who have the blessings we want and a pride which causes us to think we are more worthy of such blessings than those around us. Envy keeps us from being able to "rejoice with those who rejoice" (Rom. 12:15).

Perhaps you try to avoid married family or friends so you won't have to think about your lack of "marital bliss."[43] Or maybe you make up excuses in order to avoid attending a good friend's wedding because it will be too painful for you. Maybe you are tempted to envy what God has given them or to resent their marriage.

Proverbs 14:30 says, "A tranquil heart gives life to the flesh, but envy makes the bones rot." Envy has a horrible internal effect on us. It eats us up from the inside. The opposite of envy, the cure, is not a change in marital status. It is "a tranquil heart." A tranquil heart is one which is at rest and peace. It isn't clawing after what others have. The result is a

---

[42] Bridges, Jerry. *Respectable Sins: Confronting the Sins we Tolerate* (Colorado Springs, CO: Navpress, 2007), pg. 149.

[43] I understand that Christian love calls your married friends and family to be considerate of your thoughts and feelings. It is true that you will face insensitive remarks and be placed in challenging circumstances. You will need God's grace to humbly and patiently respond.

freedom to really live and enjoy the life God has assigned to you.

How does one cultivate such a heart? We are free to be tranquil when we stop trying to play God. When we stop assuming we know better than God when it comes to how and when to distribute His gifts. Ultimately, the tranquil heart is one which humbly trusts the sovereign, wise, and good Father. That is what brings rest and life to the flesh (see also Ps.131).

Pride

As I have noted, a sin closely associated with envy is pride. In my pride, I think I deserve better than what I have, therefore, I envy the blessings others receive. But, there are other dangers when it comes to pride. Let's turn our attention to these dangers.

There are two sides of the "pride coin." One is what we typically think about when we hear the word *pride*. That is an arrogant, boastful individual. Perhaps you think there is no one good enough or godly enough or beautiful enough for you. You may not say it that way. You are simply looking for your "soul mate" or "the perfect 10." Or maybe you are more modest and just want someone whom you think measures up to whatever you are on the "wonderful scale" (perhaps an 8.5?). Not just any guy or girl will do. You have your checklist.

It is not wrong to have standards for those you would consider marrying. The Bible even gives you some direction in this area, but the biblical checklist is actually pretty short.

Basically, they must be a Christian who is evidencing true, saving faith and a member of the opposite sex.[44] Pride, however, adds more and more things to the list and makes the focus your own selfish desires (cf. Phil 2:3-4). Humility will seek biblical wisdom in deciding who to date and marry, but it also seeks to love another person in spite of his or her flaws.[45]

So, what we have just considered is the pride of arrogance or boasting. But this is not the only way pride is manifested. Here is how Pastor John Piper describes the different manifestations of pride:

> Boasting is the response of pride to success. Self-pity is the response of pride to suffering. Boasting says, 'I deserve admiration because I have achieved so much.' Self-pity says, 'I deserve admiration because I have sacrificed so much.' Boasting is the voice of pride in the heart of the strong. Self-pity is the voice of pride in the heart of the weak. ... The need self-pity feels does not

---

[44] There are other issues that it would be wise to consider (ex. what are their goals in life? Do they have a track record of handling conflict biblically?). Also, if there is a previous divorce, there is more to be considered. A good article on this whole subject is "Should We Get Married? Five Pre-Engagement Questions to Ask Yourselves" by David Powlison and John Yenchko (found in the Journal of Biblical Counseling Vol. 14.3 Spring 1996. Also available in a booklet form from CCEF).

[45] Don't misunderstand. I am not advocating dating or marrying someone who has serious, un-dealt with sin issues. A godly relationship is centered on God, and until individuals considering marriage deal with major patterns of sin, they will not be in close communion with God.

come from a sense of unworthiness, but from a sense of unrecognized worthiness.[46]

Let's think for a minute about self-pity. This type of pride boasts in pain. When you hear a married friend speak of his or her struggles with children do you begin to think, "I would love to have those problems instead of my loneliness"? Isn't that just comparing one form of difficulty with another in a way that makes your own problems seem better (or really worse)? Such pride keeps you from "weeping with those who weep" (Rom. 12:15).

Or perhaps this pride comes out when a family member or church member tries to encourage you, and your thought is, "You don't understand my situation." And that might be true. Maybe they haven't taken the time to understand. Maybe they don't understand *experientially,* but wouldn't a humble heart respond by listening and reflecting on what they say?

The solution is to begin by noting where you are struggling with pride. If it is boasting, recognize that every good thing you have is from God (James 1:17). Furthermore, the good traits you have are to be used for God's glory and the good of others. Spend some time meditating on Philippians 2:1-7, and then look for and be aware of areas where you are looking out for your own interests above the interests of others.

> So if there is any encouragement in Christ, any comfort
> from love, any participation in the Spirit, any affection
> and sympathy, complete my joy by being of the same
> mind, having the same love, being in full accord and of

---

[46] *Desiring God: Meditations of a Christian Hedonist* (Sisters, OR: Multnomah Publishers, 2003), pg. 302.

one mind. Do nothing from selfish ambition or conceit, but in humility count others more significant than yourselves. Let each of you look not only to his own interests, but also to the interests of others. Have this mind among yourselves, which is yours in Christ Jesus, who, though he was in the form of God, did not count equality with God a thing to be grasped, but emptied himself, by taking the form of a servant, being born in the likeness of men (Phil. 2:1-7).

If your pride is in the form of self-pity, then realize that your weaknesses are intended to put Christ on display. The Lord told Paul that the weaknesses He gave Paul were intended to highlight God's power and grace.

> But he said to me, "My grace is sufficient for you, for my power is made perfect in weakness." Therefore I will boast all the more gladly of my weaknesses, so that the power of Christ may rest upon me. For the sake of Christ, then, I am content with weaknesses, insults, hardships, persecutions, and calamities. For when I am weak, then I am strong (2 Cor. 12:9-10).

Do you believe God's strength is enough to sustain you in this trying time? Are you able to say that "for the sake of Christ…I am content with weaknesses," knowing you will experience His sustaining strength? [47]

---

[47] For help in battling pride, check out Stuart Scott's booklet *From Pride to Humility* or CJ Mahaney's book *Humility: True Greatness*.

5

The Dangers of Worldliness

Have you ever been to another country? I have been to a few and every time I am quickly reminded that I am in a place very different from home. The language, cultural icons, sights, and smells are all so different.

In a similar way, we must realize that we Christians are not in our home country. We are strangers in this fallen world. Our citizenship is in heaven. Therefore, we are to live in this world, but we are to be strangers in it. We are not to

> love the world or the things in the world...for all that
> is in the world—the desires of the flesh and the
> desires of the eyes and pride of life—is not from the
> Father but is from the world (1 John 2:15-16).

"World," in this passage, refers to the ways of thinking and acting which are in opposition to godly ways of thinking and behaving. So, we are not to love or embrace ways of thinking and living which are contrary to God's Word. We are to live as citizens of the Kingdom of God rather than citizens of the domain of darkness. We are ambassadors, or representatives, of God to the world.

In this chapter we will consider two areas where all Christians, and especially unmarried Christians, are tempted to live in ways which contradict their true citizenship. The first is having a worldly perspective about relationships with members of the opposite sex. The second is the temptation towards sexual immorality.

Worldly Perspective on Relationships

How does the world's thinking about relationships differ from the biblical view? The worldly thinking we encounter in the United States is that relationships are some sort of game. It is common to single out someone of the opposite sex for an intimate friendship or dating relationship with no thought of marriage. Dating is simply a way to have fun and enjoy the companionship of a member of the opposite sex.

This, however, does not fit with the biblical picture. For starters, how does this model Christian love? Christ came to serve, not to be served. The "just have fun" model of dating is not focused on serving one another. It is, instead, enjoying the benefits of relationship with no desire to move towards the formal commitment of marriage.

"Formal commitment!? That seems to stifle love," you might think. However, I would argue that it is the context in which true love flourishes and is enjoyed. Look at God's love towards us. He doesn't just "go with the flow." He intentionally pursues us. He makes a covenant, a formal promise, to have us as His people. And in this context we can bask in His love and have no reason to think He will abandon us. If we are to reflect God instead of the world, such a formal commitment must be the aim and goal of any dating relationship.

Additionally, spending regular one-on-one time with a member of the opposite sex (whether you call it dating or not) is not loving.[48] For one thing, one or both of you probably hope that this relationship is heading somewhere beyond friendship. This is probably the case even if you both verbalize a desire to "just be friends."

Even if it were true that you both really *only* wanted to be close friends it is not loving, because, to put it crassly, it takes the other person "off the market." What I mean is that it keeps other potential men from pursuing her and causes other potential women to assume he is not interested in them. It appears to outsiders that you are an "item," so no one else makes a move and everyone is confused. Even if you tell people that you and your friend are not an item, you must wonder if a prospective date would be interested in being with you while you are closely relating to another member of the opposite sex. I am sure my wife would not be happy if I did that, and I think the same would go for those who are pursuing marriage. It seems like a double standard to argue otherwise.

You may argue, "But I have Christian freedom since no Bible verse prohibits this type of recreational dating." I

---

[48] Some may justify it by the fact that the other person wants this type of relationship too. However, this is not the litmus test for what type of behavior is becoming for a citizen of heaven. Rather, the true test of love is found in what God says Christian love looks like.

would say that the biblical principles of love do oppose such relationships. Paul said in Galatians 3:3-4,

> For you were called to freedom, brothers. Only do not use your freedom as an opportunity for the flesh, but through love serve one another. For the whole law is fulfilled in one word: 'You shall love your neighbor as yourself.'

If what I have said is true, then you must honestly ask yourself if your intimate friendships with members of the opposite sex are actually a loving service to one another.

Let me be clear. I am not saying that you cannot be friends and show Christian love to members of the opposite sex. I am saying that you cannot be *close, intimate* friends with a member of the opposite sex without being either foolish or selfish.[49]

If you desire such companionship, then pursue the security of a marriage covenant to enjoy such intimacy. If you do not desire marriage, then develop friendships with members of the same sex who can hold you accountable and encourage you in your walk with the Lord. Then, find ways to serve members of the opposite sex that do not single them out unnecessarily. Spend time in groups studying the Bible, praying, serving, and socializing.

---

[49] To clarify, by "close, intimate friend," I mean someone who spend a lot of one-on-one time with, share your deepest feelings, thoughts, and desires with, etc.

Sexual Sin and Impurity

As Christians, we are to display God's character to one another and a watching world, therefore holiness is not optional for the Christian. We are ambassadors of the holy God of the universe, so we must be holy. Such holiness means living within the guidelines God has given us for sexuality and purity. Holiness involves more than that, but it is surely not less than that. In the season of singleness, temptations towards sexual sin can be strong. So, we would do well to prepare for facing them.

That God calls Christians, married and single, to sexual fidelity and purity is clear in Scripture. Here is one example from 1 Thessalonians 4:3-8:

> For this is the will of God, your sanctification: that you ***abstain from sexual immorality***; that each one of you know how to control his own body in holiness and honor, not in the passion of lust like the Gentiles who do not know God; ***that no one transgress and wrong his brother in this matter,*** because the Lord is an avenger in all these things, as we told you beforehand and solemnly warned you. ***For God has not called us for impurity, but in holiness.*** Therefore whoever disregards this, disregards not man but God, who gives his Holy Spirit to you.

Verse six says that we must not "transgress and wrong" one another in the matter of purity. To transgress is to go beyond the proper limits of behavior. The Greek word for "wrong" means "to take advantage of, exploit, outwit, defraud, or cheat someone."[50]

---

[50]"πλεονεκτέω" in Arndt, W., Danker, F. W., & Bauer, W. *A Greek-English lexicon of the New Testament and other early Christian literature* (3rd ed.). Accessed in Logos Bible software.

To engage in sexual immorality or to look lustfully (or desire to have others think you look sexy) is to take advantage of others. It is to take what does not belong to you for selfish gain. This is the case whether it is their body or their special attention which should belong only to a (future) spouse. This is the opposite of biblical love. Rosaria Butterfield puts it well when she writes,

> God is calling us to so greatly love others that we do not desire for them anything that might separate them from God. Holy sexuality is a love so big that it treasures the purity of another, exonerating that person's status as an image bearer or a daughter or son of the King, and not dehumanizing him or her through manipulating lust.[51]

How Can You Avoid Defrauding Someone?

When it comes to sexual behavior, we are to relate in appropriate ways based on the relationships we have. Paul tells Timothy to treat older women like mothers and younger women like sisters, with all purity (1 Tim. 5:2). He tells Titus to make sure the older women instruct the younger women to be pure (Titus 2:5).

This means that if you are a man, every woman who is not your wife, even if she is your girlfriend or fiancée, is in the category of "sister." If you are a woman, every man who is not your husband is your "brother." There is not a special category in which you can take the physical to the next level simply because you are "more committed" to each other. There is no category of "friend with benefits." Being engaged does not change the fact that you are still unmarried. Your relationship is that of brother and sister.

---

[51] *Openness Unhindered: Further Thoughts of an Unlikely Convert on Sexual Identity and Union with Christ.* Kindle edition chapter 3.

Thinking that physical intimacy is simply commensurate to your level of commitment fails to understand the biblical view of marriage and sexuality. And what is the biblical understanding of sex and marriage?

Sex is part of God's good design for marriage. Marriage and sexuality are intended to put Jesus and his bride, the Church, on display.[52] This is why fornication[53] is so wrong. Read what theologian Dr. Russell Moore says about it:

> Fornication isn't merely "premarital." Premarital is the language of timing, and with it we infer that this is simply the marital act misfired at the wrong time. But fornication is, both spiritually and typologically, a different sort of act from the marital act. That's why the consequences are so dire.
>
> Fornication pictures a different reality than the mystery of Christ presented in the one-flesh union of covenantal marriage. It represents a Christ who uses his church without joining her, covenantally and permanently, to himself. The man who leads a woman into sexual union without a covenantal bond is preaching to her, to the world, and to himself a different gospel from the gospel of Jesus Christ. And he is forming a real spiritual union, the Apostle Paul warns, but one with a different spirit than the Spirit of Christ (1 Cor. 6:15, 19).[54]

---

[52]There are other ways we put Christ on display. So, those who are single do not need to fear they will be unable to put Christ on display if they never marry. The single shows Christ by living a life that is undivided in devotion to Christ. Having joy in Christ and his kingdom, even when your own kingdom (family) is not being built puts the glory and worthiness of Christ on display to a world that only looks at the physical. See chapters 1-2 and the conclusion.

[53] See 1 Cor. 6:9 NASB, Heb. 13:4 NASB. Fornication is the biblical word for sexual immorality between unmarried people.

[54]"Premarital Sex?", Accessed at www.russellmoore.com on June 6, 2013.

So, what is sex, biblically speaking? *Sex is the God-honoring, service to your spouse that is the sign of your covenant relationship.* Sex is the *sign* of the covenant. It reveals the covenant reality that the two are one flesh.

Now, granted that sex is sinful for those who are not married, how should our level of physical intimacy look prior to marriage? Is it OK to become more physically involved as our dating relationship progresses (as long as we avoid "going all the way")? Is our physical intimacy proportionate to our level of commitment, finally reaching intercourse once we make the ultimate level of commitment?

I would argue that, given what we have said about the design and purpose of sex, the answer to those questions is a resounding "No!" I say this for several reasons.

First, physical intimacy is designed to lead towards sex. This is why a married couple calls things like passionate kissing "foreplay." It is the on-ramp to the highway of intercourse. On-ramps are not designed for U-turns. They lead in one direction and are intended for acceleration.

Second, since sex is reserved for marriage, and since the Bible commands us to treat each other as sisters and brothers prior to marriage, physical intimacy levels do not increase as we move towards marriage. Instead, it stays at the level of brother and sister until after the covenant of marriage is enacted. At that point the sign of the covenant is joyfully expressed. This may seem a little abstract, so let me help with two graphs I created based on an illustration I heard from Michael Lawrence.[55]

---

[55] This is from a talk that Mark Dever, Michael Lawrence, Scott Croft, and Matt Schmucker gave at a Desiring God conference. The talk was entitled, "Sex and the Single Man" and is available at www.desiringgod.org.

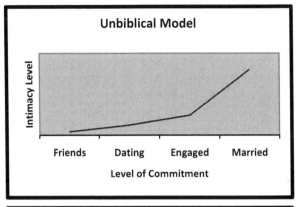

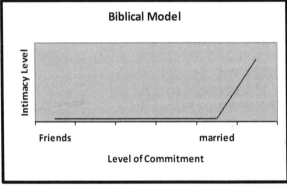

In the first graph, we see the common perspective that intimacy increases as level of commitment increases. In the second, we see the biblical perspective. In this view, you treat one another as siblings until the marriage covenant, which testifies to the gospel of Jesus Christ, is enacted.

So, on a practical level, what type of physical interactions are appropriate? A good principle is to ask, "Is this something I would do with my flesh and blood brother or sister?" If the answer is "No," then neither should you be doing it with one whom the Bible says is your brother or sister. That is why Paul says to treat women whom you are not married to as mothers or sisters, with absolute purity (1 Tim. 5:2).

Does this sound radical? I think it might but not because it is untrue and incorrect. I think the reason it sounds radical is that we live in a culture which seems to deify relationships and sexuality. As Christians, we may see through many of the lies, but I wonder if we have been swayed more in this area by the world than by the Bible.

So, we must not commit fornication or engage in increasing levels of physical intimacy as our dating relationships progress, but that is not all the Bible says about sexual purity.

Purity in Thoughts

We must also avoid the impurity of *looking* lustfully at others. Jesus said that this is the same as committing adultery because God sees not just our actions but our heart (Matt. 5:28). Holiness, then, requires purity in action *and thought*. And this extends to what we watch on TV, what we look at on the computer, what we read, and what we think.[56] As Romans 13:14 says, we are to "put on the Lord Jesus Christ, and make no provision for the flesh, to gratify its desires."

Conclusion

Does your view of sexuality line up with God's purposes for it? Or are you tempted to believe the lies of the world? Will you trust the goodness of God and His design or will you trust the yearnings of your appetites (i.e., "it feels good so it must be right")?

I realize that some reading this may be filled with regret. Perhaps you have failed to live up to God's standards of holiness in your past or current relationship. Remember that

---

[56] If you struggle with sexual temptation (including pornography or masturbation), I recommend reading Josh Harris' book *Sex is Not the Problem (Lust is).*

God's grace does not ask you to undo the past. God's grace calls you to rest fully in the righteous record of Jesus for you. It also changes you and enables you to be shaped progressively into the image of your righteous Christ (Titus 3:3-8). Repent before God and one another and pursue holiness by God's grace.

Brothers and sisters, beware that you do not imbibe the world's philosophies (Jer. 2:13). We ought to think carefully about what Christian love looks like in all of our relationships and see where worldly or selfish thinking has crept in. You are strangers in a foreign land. You are citizens of heaven, and the ways of the world should often times look just as strange as the cultural differences you might experience when you visit another country. As citizens of God's Kingdom we must be those who put God's holiness and love on display.

6

The Dangers of Fear and Failing to Steward Time Well

Regret is a powerful word. It conjures up thoughts of loss, waste, and failure. While we all will probably have some sense of regret, I would hope to spare you it in the areas of wasted time and energy. Some of the greatest regrets that many older folks have revolve around past anxieties and poor stewardship of time and opportunities. Looking back on life it becomes clear that anxiety over the future actually sapped the life right out of the present – it wasted away strength and joy. It also becomes apparent that time wasted on unimportant things or being so busy that one could not focus on what really mattered devoured productive years of life and service to God. Let's take a moment to look at the temptations towards anxiety and poor stewardship of time so that we might be equipped to resist them.

Anxiety and Fear Concerning the Future

Anxious thoughts can often present themselves in the following manner, "What if [insert some bad outcome] happens?" Fear takes that "what if…" thought and changes it into a statement such as, "I *know* this bad thing will happen, and I am fearful of it." Perhaps you have found yourself tempted to worry and be fearful in this single period of life.

Maybe you are anxious that you will scare away Mr. or Miss Right. This leads you to constantly replay conversations you have had with potential dates and analyze everything that was said. Such anxiety ties you up in knots. Internally, you always feel nervous. Externally, you are not able to minister to those around you because you are so concerned with avoiding your worst fears – a further protracted state of singleness – that you are unable to genuinely care about those around you. Those of the opposite sex become either potential spouses or rejects rather than brothers and sisters to care for and serve with no strings attached.

Or maybe you are tempted to fear what the future will be like if the Lord never gives you a spouse. As a single woman you might be anxious about anything from how to take care of maintenance issues to who will to take care of you as you age. As a man you may fear lonely nights at home by yourself.

What is the cure? For starters, I would suggest reading Matthew 6:25-34 (though starting in v. 19 is a good idea).

> Therefore I tell you, do not be anxious about your life, what you will eat or what you will drink, nor about your

body, what you will put on. Is not life more than food, and the body more than clothing? Look at the birds of the air: they neither sow nor reap nor gather into barns, and yet your heavenly Father feeds them. Are you not of more value than they? And which of you by being anxious can add a single hour to his span of life? And why are you anxious about clothing? Consider the lilies of the field, how they grow: they neither toil nor spin, yet I tell you, even Solomon in all his glory was not arrayed like one of these. But if God so clothes the grass of the field, which today is alive and tomorrow is thrown into the oven, will he not much more clothe you, O you of little faith? Therefore do not be anxious, saying, 'What shall we eat?' or 'What shall we drink?' or 'What shall we wear?' For the Gentiles seek after all these things, and your heavenly Father knows that you need them all. But seek first the kingdom of God and his righteousness, and all these things will be added to you.

Therefore do not be anxious about tomorrow, for tomorrow will be anxious for itself. Sufficient for the day is its own trouble.

In this passage, Jesus speaks to crowds of people who had many "good" reasons to worry. For example, a drought could mean *no* food and subsequent starvation. This is not like today when we can just ship food in from thousands of miles away. But even in such a precarious spot, Jesus gives them better reasons not to worry. Take some time to read that passage and note the reasons He gives. For now, I want to look at the reason Jesus gives for why we worry.

The main reason we give in to the temptation to worry is that we have "little faith" (Matt. 6:30). It is not necessarily that we have "no faith." What we need is a larger view of the God who cares. He oversees, in splendid fashion, the smallest parts of His creation. How much more will He oversee your life and care for you? He knows what you need.

As the years go by and you remain single, you may be tempted to worry that you will never be married or have children. Realize that God's plans are not thwarted by the passage of time; rather, all things unfold in His timing. So, do not be anxious, for which of you can add a wedding ring to your hand by worrying?

Failing to be Faithful in Regards to Time

Every ounce of energy and every moment of time is a gift from God. Being unmarried may provide you with more freedom over how you will use your time.[57] You have more flexibility as to how you will use your time. With this freedom comes temptations. There are two main ways of falling into temptation in this area.

The first temptation is that of being selfish with your time. Paul explicitly says that one of the benefits of remaining unmarried is that a person is free from the cares and responsibilities of fulfilling martial roles so that he or she can demonstrate the glory of God in another way (1 Cor. 7:32-35). That way is undivided devotion to the Lord. In other words, the single person has fewer specific requirements as to how he or she must use time and energy. But, do not mistake this for freedom to do *whatever you want* with *your* time. No, it is the Lord's time (just as it is for the married person).

---

[57] This is obviously not the case if you are a single parent or are caring for aging parents.

Perhaps you are really enjoying being single *because* you are able to do what you want to do when you want to do it. If what you want to do, however, is selfish, that is an unbiblical reason to stay single. Such an approach is the opposite of what Paul describes in 1 Corinthians 7. If your free time is only filled with leisure activities and lazy days then you need to ask God to give you more of a zeal for His Kingdom and ministry to others.

Now, don't get confused by this and go to the other extreme. *The other extreme is failing to be faithful to God by over-committing.* This is saying, "Yes" to every request you get without examining how to use your time best to glorify God. Maybe you feel like every waking moment must be spent *doing* and *going.* However, this is not the biblical picture. This approach to life arises from either a fear of disappointing others or a disorganized life rather than an undistracted devotion to the Lord.

Let me give you some examples. Perhaps you become so busy working, vacationing, or even serving that you become unfaithful in your personal spiritual growth. Or maybe you fail to serve others well because you are investing in too many people at once. You are unable to really have an impact because you are stretched too thin. Or maybe you do so much that you never rest.[58]

---

[58] It is pride if you do not think you need rest. You are a finite creature, not the omnipotent Creator. Our need for rest humbles us by forcing us to recognize, in a tangible way, that we are dependent on the only One who is self-sufficient. It is fear of man if you know you need to stop and rest but fear letting others down if you say "no." In this case, you care more about what others think than what God requires of you.

If you are struggling with your use of time, let me suggest getting a godly friend to help you evaluate your schedule. If you are being selfish, ask him or her to help you think of ways to serve God and others with your time and energy. If you are over-committing, ask him or her to help you evaluate your current commitments and make adjustments. You may even ask him or her to help you consider future requests that people will make of your time.

Fight Temptation

At this point you may be weighed down by all the ways you have given into temptation in these areas. Or you could be congratulating yourself for how well you are doing. Let me encourage you to avoid both of those responses.

We are to feel guilty over sin, but we are not to wallow in such guilt. We have a faithful and righteous High Priest who lived the perfect life that God requires. He did this on our behalf! He died to pay the penalty for our sins. He is seated at the right hand of the Father to be our advocate. So, draw near to the throne of grace (Hebrews 4:14-16). Confess your sins and ask for renewed strength to live in light of the new life you already have in Christ (Rom. 6:1-14).

If you think you are doing well, give glory to God. It is Christ who is at work in you to do what God commands (Phil. 2:13). And remember that if you think you stand you should take heed lest you fall (1 Cor. 10:12). At some point you will probably be tempted in at least one of these areas. Humbly ask God to help you resist temptation.

Along the way, I have given some *specific* ways to combat particular temptations. I want to conclude this section by giving a few *general* principles for battling all of the temptations I have mentioned so far.

Meditate on God's Grace

First, reflect on God's love for you in Christ. The gospel is where you most clearly see the sovereignty, goodness, and wisdom of God towards you. He sovereignly comes to show you His goodness through the wisdom of the gospel message. Understanding and believing the gospel generates a loving and humble trust in God which pushes sinful desires out of the heart.

This is not a one-time act, and it does not come naturally to our hearts. If you do not make this a conscious, ongoing effort, it will not happen. Plan to meditate on passages of Scripture such as:

> **Romans 8:32** He who did not spare his own Son but gave him up for us all, how will he not also with him graciously give us all things?

> **Ephesians 2:1-10** And you were dead in the trespasses and sins in which you once walked, following the course of this world, following the prince of the power of the air, the spirit that is now at work in the sons of disobedience— among whom we all once lived in the passions of our flesh, carrying out the desires of the body and the mind, and were by nature children of wrath, like the rest of mankind. But God, being rich in mercy, because of the great love with which he loved us, even when we were dead in our trespasses, made us alive

together with Christ—by grace you have been saved—
and raised us up with him and seated us with him in the
heavenly places in Christ Jesus, so that in the coming ages
he might show the immeasurable riches of his grace in
kindness toward us in Christ Jesus. For by grace you have
been saved through faith. And this is not your own doing;
it is the gift of God, not a result of works, so that no one
may boast. For we are his workmanship, created in Christ
Jesus for good works, which God prepared beforehand,
that we should walk in them.

Titus 3:3-8 For we ourselves were once foolish,
disobedient, led astray, slaves to various passions and
pleasures, passing our days in malice and envy, hated by
others and hating one another. But when the goodness
and loving kindness of God our Savior appeared, he saved
us, not because of works done by us in righteousness, but
according to his own mercy, by the washing of
regeneration and renewal of the Holy Spirit, whom he
poured out on us richly through Jesus Christ our Savior, so
that being justified by his grace we might become heirs
according to the hope of eternal life. The saying is
trustworthy, and I want you to insist on these things, so
that those who have believed in God may be careful to
devote themselves to good works. These things are
excellent and profitable for people.

Put off Sin and Put on Righteousness

While meditating on such wonderful truths, begin to
prayerfully and actively replace sinful behavior with a
lifestyle that honors God. So, for example, think of ways to
put off manifestations of pride and how to put on humility.

There are many good books that address each of the areas of temptation mentioned above. It may be helpful for you to ask your pastor or an older godly man or woman at your church to help you pick out some good materials. [59]

Benefit from Your Church Family

That brings me to my final point. Benefit from your church family. Even though you may be single with regard to marital status, you are not alone when it comes to fighting sin. God has placed you in a body of believers. Faithfully gather with a local church to worship God, encourage one another, and reach out to the lost. Share your struggles with a trusted Christian friend of the same sex. Ask for their accountability and encouragement.

---

[59] For a fuller treatment on growing in godliness check out *How Can I Change?* By CJ Mahaney and Robert Boisvert and the CCEF mini-booklet *Temptation: Fighting the Urge* by Tim Lane (CCEF has other great mini-booklets on specific issues. Visit www.ccef.org).

Section Three:

Living in the Single Season

Honoring God as a single person

7

Honoring God by Maturing as a Christian Man or Woman

Have you ever played Chutes and Ladders? It's the game where you move from start to finish on a game board and at times skip many spaces by taking a ladder or fall back many spaces by landing on a chute (slide). Perhaps you have taken a ladder to get here. You may have just skipped ahead to this section without reading the earlier chapters. You might be thinking, "Who needs all this theology, and who wants to hear all this stuff about sin? Give me the practical, how-to stuff." If that is you, consider this present admonition a chute taking you back to the beginning.

The most important thing about you is what you believe about God. It informs the way you think and live and seek a spouse. In other words, all the "how-to" stuff is firmly based on foundational truths about and from God. If you don't have those, then ultimately no amount of "how-to" stuff will be of benefit to you.

How to Prepare for Marriage

I often have young, single men ask me what they should do to prepare for marriage. Such a question encourages me. They want to honor God and serve their future wife. The funny thing about preparing for marriage is that it is, in many ways, nothing more than maturing as a Christian. So, in one sense, every single Christian is not preparing for marriage, but simply maturing as a Christian. That being said, there are also some thoughts which do apply more specifically to single Christians who desire marriage.

So, how do I respond to those who ask how to prepare for marriage? My response is five-fold. They need to:

1. Grow in godly character,
2. Learn biblical masculinity and femininity,
3. Join and serve a healthy local church,
4. Prepare to leave mother and father,
5. Seek a spouse in ways that demonstrate faith in God and love towards others.

The first three apply to every Christian, even if they have no desire for marriage. I will expand on those in this chapter and then look at the more practical issues related to preparing for marriage in the following two chapters.

Before I do that, however, let me mention that this is not a "five-step plan to marriage." There is no such thing. God gives us no "steps" to marriage. Doing these things does not mean God will owe you a spouse. God's grace and gifts are not something we work to earn. By definition they are undeserved. So don't try to make God a debtor to you. He does not and will not owe you anything, but He does freely and mercifully show you His goodness. His mercies are new every morning whether they include a spouse or not. Do not take these five things as steps to get what you want or ways to manipulate God, rather see them as ways you delight in and honor God while trusting His sovereign, wise, and good plans for you.

Grow in Godly Character

Every Christian, single or married, is called to live a godly life (1 Tim. 4:7). So, my first piece of counsel to someone living in the single season is to make it their aim to glorify God by looking more and more like Jesus. This is not something we can do by our own power. We are not saved by works, and we will not be conformed to the image of Christ by simply working harder (Gal. 3:3). This doesn't mean we just "let go and let God" do the work of growth for us. Our sanctification does involve us working with God's empowering grace.[60]

Paul brings these two ideas into clear view when he says,

> work out your own salvation with fear and trembling, for it is God who works in you, both to will and to work for his good pleasure (Phil. 2:12b-13).

Do you see both truths there? He commands us to "work out [our] salvation." Notice he doesn't say "work *for* your salvation." He basically says, "God saves you from the power of sin, now work out the implications of this freedom

---

[60] Justification, on the other hand, is a work which we do not cooperate in. It is wholly of God. See Ephesians 1:11 and Romans 8:29-30.

in your life." You must work to put off sin and put on righteousness. But, this "working" is not a "pull yourself up by your bootstraps," self-empowered change. Paul says the reason you work out your salvation is because "it is God who works in you." He is working in us to incline our will to do the things which please Him.

With that groundwork laid, it is time to think of specific areas where you may need to grow. We don't fall into godliness. We must pursue it. And we don't change in generalities; we change in specifics. What I mean is that we don't change by saying, "I need to grow in Christ-likeness." We change when we ask, "In what specific areas do I need to look more like Christ?" Then, we look to the Bible to see the character that is becoming of one who has new life in Christ.

To help you think specifically and biblically about areas of character to grow in, I suggest you start by holding up Titus 1:7-9 as a mirror to your life. Here Paul lays out the qualifications for elder. You may think, "But I'm not asking to be an elder, just a godly man." Or you may be thinking, "I am a woman, how does this apply to me?" It applies because every Christian is called to live a life characterized by these virtues and absent of these vices.[61]

Let's examine these qualifications for a moment. The main charge is to be **above reproach**. This is to live with a clear conscience before God and man. Paul fleshes this out with a list of five vices to put off and six virtues to put on so that you will be godly. Below, I have a chart showing the vices

---

[61] All of them, with the exception of "able to teach," are found either directly or indirectly in other passages as characteristics for all Christians to exhibit.

(and the opposite characteristic to put on) as well as a chart describing the virtues. I encourage you to look for specific areas where you can focus on growing. Remember, change won't happen in the general. So get specific as to where you need to grow and what growth will look like.

Five Vices to Replace

Vice	Opposite	Application
Arrogance/Self-will- Pushy and seeking one's own will instead of God's and instead of looking out for the interests of others. It is also a pride that won't receive criticism well.	A humble servant who looks out for the interest of others instead of using power for personal gain (Matt. 20:25-28). A proper view of self (a sinner) which enables you to receive criticism.	Do you often push for your own way? How are you looking out for the interests of others? How do you handle criticism? Do you examine it humbly to see if it is true or does it go "in one ear and out the other?"
Quick-Tempered- Having a "short fuse," or being easily angered.	Humility, gentleness, patience, love (Eph. 4:1-2).	Are you easily provoked to anger by people and situations? If you ask someone to do something and they don't do it the way you want or they fail, how do you respond? With patience or in anger?
Drunkard- A person whose companion is wine (or any other substance that causes a person to not be clear-headed/sober-minded).	Being self-controlled and filled with the Spirit (Eph. 4:18).	Are you free not to drink? Do you drink to the point of not being clear-headed? Do you see alcohol as a means of escaping life's problems?

Violent- Abusiveness, meanness, or fighting to get one's own way or to suppress opposition. Riding rough-shod over others or bullying them with physical violence or with your words.	Gentleness (1 Tim 3:3) and being a peacemaker (Rom. 12:18).	Do you like brawling to get your way (physically or striking with your words)? Are you argumentative or quick to attack those who get in your way or express a different opinion? Or, do you seek peace in situations?
Greedy for Gain- Seeking financial or material gain without integrity. Loving money and material things. Unsatisfied with what you have.	Contentment (1 Tim. 6:6), seeking God's Kingdom and His righteousness above all (Matt. 6). Being a cheerful giver (2 Cor. 9:7).	Are you content financially and materially? Or do you constantly seek happiness in having newer and nicer things (phones, clothes, etc.)?

Six Virtues to Put on

Virtue	Application
Hospitable- One who gives practical help to new comers.	Are you welcoming new people at church instead of just talking to your group of friends? Do you try to meet the needs of other Christians that you do not know that well? Or are you quick to make excuses and slow to inconvenience yourself for others?
Loving what is good- Loves what is good as opposed to sinful, worthless, and not God-glorifying.	Our close friendships should be with those who love good things. The ultimate "good" is Christ. So you should love those who love Christ. Do the TV shows you watch make light of that which is evil according to God? The problem is not that

	you would go *do* the things you see, but that you are mentally delighting in what is not good.
Sensible- Being wise and thoughtful. Not being driven by emotion, but cool-headed.	Are you controlled in your thinking, not given to a lack of control and being "feelings" driven?
Upright- Living righteously and justly.	Do you seek to practice righteousness in your everyday life? Do you want to be just in your dealings with others?
Holy/Devout- Living a life that is pleasing to God.	Do you regularly confess and repent of your sin before the Lord (even if others don't know about it)? Do you seek to find out what pleases the Lord from His Word? Do you seek to do what is pleasing to the Lord?
Disciplined/ Self-controlled- Having one's desires in check and under control.	Are you ruled by your desires for money, sleep (laziness), food (overeating), and/or material things? Do you lack control with your use of time (wasting much time on TV or the Internet) or money? Or do you rule over your desires so that you might be focused on pursuing the one prize-namely, Jesus (1 Cor. 9:24-27)?

Have you found a few areas to grow in? Please, do not move on without taking some time for honest, humble self-evaluation.

Learn Biblical Masculinity and Femininity

That brings us to point number two. Every Christian, no matter his or her marital status, must grow in a biblical sense of masculinity and femininity. This may sound rather foreign in our egalitarian society which says that there is no difference between men and women. Our culture is quick to steamroll any distinctions between men and women because they think differences mean inequality. But, we must think biblically on this issue.

In His wisdom, God has designed men and women to complement one another (not compliment- though that isn't a bad thing to do). That is, He has made them equal, yet different. Men and women are *equal* in their dignity as humans (Gen. 1:26-27), their need and path to salvation (Rom. 3:23, Gal. 3:27-29), and their ability to possess spiritual gifts (Rom. 12:3-8).[62]

Men and women are *different* in their roles. So what are the differences? Here is how John Piper summarizes what the Bible says about mature masculinity and femininity:

> At the heart of mature masculinity is a sense of benevolent responsibility to lead, provide for and protect

---

[62] Note, a woman can be gifted by the Spirit of God to teach. This does not mean she should use this gift in a way which violates the Spirit's clear directions in Scripture for a woman not to be a teacher of the Word of God to men (see. 1 Tim. 2:12). She should exercise this gift in other, God-honoring ways (teaching children's Sunday school, teaching other women, etc.).

women in ways appropriate to a man's differing relationships. [63]

At the heart of mature femininity is a freeing disposition to affirm, receive and nurture strength and leadership from worthy men in ways appropriate to a woman's differing relationships.[64]

There is a lot packed in to these definitions. If this is brand new to you I encourage you to read Piper's chapter entitled "A Vision of Biblical Complementarity" in the book *Recovering Biblical Manhood and Womanhood.*[65] In that chapter, he unpacks each of these phrases. For now, I will point out a few of the key differences.

Mature masculinity is a responsibility to lead (Eph. 5:23).[66] It is not a "right" but a weighty responsibility (Luke 22:24-27). It is not self-seeking, but seeking what is best for those you are leading (Mark 10:45). Mature masculinity is also providing for and protecting (Eph. 5:25, 28-29). That involves taking initiative and not being passive. All of these things are to be done for the women around you in ways which are appropriate to your relationship with them (it looks different depending on if they are your mother, sister, wife,

---

[63] John Piper, in *Recovering Biblical Manhood and Womanhood,* Ed. John Piper & Wayne Grudem (Wheaton, IL: Crossway Books, 2006), pg. 36.

[64] Ibid., pg. 46

[65] This is available for free download from www.desiringgod.org.

[66] I realize many of these verses deal directly with the marriage relationship, but as John Piper argues, these roles are ingrained into our natures as men and women, and these desires and actions don't just spontaneously generate once we are married.

employee, etc.). When it comes to dating, you must be the one to take the risk and try to initiate a relationship. When it comes to the direction of the relationship, you must not simply "go with the flow" but provide direction. When it comes to purity, you must lead her in holy ways.

Mature femininity is a desire to encourage and receive this leadership, provision, and protection from godly men (Eph. 5:22). This means you are not domineering, and you are not a doormat (1 Pet. 3:1-6). You are active in responding to men in appropriate ways given your relationship with them (father, brother, husband, employee, etc.). In a dating relationship, you are not submitting to him as you would a husband, but you are looking to see if he is the kind of man you could marry and therefore submit to. You are affirming and receiving his leadership in the current relationship.

This design of equality and distinction brings God glory and causes men and women to flourish. Therefore, men and women must learn how to biblically live out their God-given roles. Obviously there is a lot more that could be said. I have not had the space to provide the biblical support for this vision of manhood and womanhood. If this is brand new thinking to you, I strongly encourage you to spend time studying this issue.[67]

---

[67] For more information on this, check out John Piper's book or DVD series entitled *What's the Difference: Manhood and Womanhood Defined According to the Bible.*

Join and Serve a Healthy Local Church

Growth in godliness and manhood or womanhood is meant to happen in discipleship relationships. What I mean is a relationship in which a young man finds a more mature, godly man to help him learn and grow and a younger woman does the same with an older woman. This is why Paul commands Titus to see to it that older men and women are instructing the younger men and women in the things we have been discussing (see Titus 2).

These discipleship relationships don't have to be formal, but they will not happen without some intentionality. First, you must be part of a local body of Christians. The New Testament knows nothing of a lone ranger Christian.[68] Second, you need to spend time with fellow church members. Third, you need to be teachable. That is you need to have a humility in which you do not assume you already know everything about the Christian life, and you must not be defensive when challenged in your thinking or behavior. Finally, you need to have open and honest discussions with a few members you are close to about your struggles, joys, and questions you have.

Not only does the local church provide the atmosphere for the growth we have mentioned to take place, it is also where you exercise your spiritual gifts. In 1 Corinthians 12:7 Paul says, "To each is given the manifestation of the Spirit for the

---

[68] Here is some evidence for that. 1. The New Testament letters are written to local churches or church leaders. 2. Commands to leaders in the church to shepherd the flock means there must be a flock to be shepherded. 3. The "one another" commands (i.e., love one another, serve one another, etc.) require you to be in constant fellowship with Christians in the church.

common good." Your gifts are not *your* gifts. They are for the good of the body of Christ -- the church. You have the responsibility to use the gifts God has given you for the health of the body of Christ. This applies even to your gift of singleness. Don't think, "Because I am single I am unimportant to the body."[69]

If you are not part of a local body of believers, why not commit to a healthy church today?[70] If you already are a member, are you exercising your gifts? Are you participating in the life of the body? Or, are you isolating yourself because of your marital status? I understand that the body of Christ often fails to make singles feel like they have a place, but, don't let that stop you from doing what God has called you to do. Don't let your perceptions or self-pity stop you from serving.

Are You Preparing for Marriage?

Every Christian must be growing in godliness, living as God designed you, and functioning in the body of Christ. These are not nice add-ons for the truly spiritual. This is simply faithful Christian living

For those of you interested in marriage, you are probably still wondering how you should go about preparing specifically for marriage. In our next chapter, we will look at the last two points which apply more specifically to the subset of Christian singles who are interested in marriage.

---

[69] 1 Cor. 12:14-15- "For the body does not consist of one member but of many. If the foot should say, 'Because I am not a hand, I do not belong to the body,' that would not make it any less a part of the body."

[70] If you need help figuring out what a healthy church looks like, according to the Bible, then check out "What are the 9 Marks?" at www.9marks.org.

8

Honoring God as You Look for a Spouse

In the last chapter I began my response to the question, "How do you prepare for marriage?" I outlined my response with these five points:

1. Grow in godly character,
2. Learn biblical masculinity and femininity,
3. Join and serve a healthy local church,
4. Prepare to leave mother and father,
5. Seek a spouse in ways that demonstrate faith in God and love towards others.

The first three items above apply to all Christians. So, the initial answer to how to prepare for marriage is to live as a godly, Christian man or woman in the context of a healthy church.

Now we turn to the last two points which deal with the more practical issues of getting ready for marriage. Remember, these are not intended to be a simple "five steps to marriage" formula. God is sovereign in the distribution of his gifts including marriage and singleness. So, these are not steps, but ways in which we honor God as we trust and wait.

Prepare to Leave Mother and Father

The fourth part of preparing for marriage is getting in a position to leave your parents and unite to a spouse. Genesis 2:24 says, "Therefore a man shall leave his father and his mother and hold fast to his wife, and they shall become one flesh." This idea of leaving father and mother to form a new family unit is part of what it means to be married. So, a young man or woman must put himself or herself in a position to do this.

This is the biblical principle, but what does it look like? In American culture, I believe this means a couple will be able to financially support themselves. You may not have enough money to buy a nice house, a car, etc. However, you should have enough income to pay for housing, transportation (even if it is the bus), and food (Ramen noodles, anyone?). Continued dependence on parents for financial support should be phasing out as you move toward marriage.

Leaving mother and father is more than just an issue of finances. I also believe this means learning to live independently in terms of decision making and emotional support. This is not the same thing as being a "know-it-all" or the foolishness of not heeding wise counsel. And it is not something that happens apart from growing in financial independence.[71] Learn how to listen to counsel and then make responsible, adult decisions. To prepare for marriage, you need to develop the ability to apply biblical principles to life decisions.

As a single person it is often wise to involve your parents in the major decisions you make.[72] This is especially true if they are Christians. They can help you see how God's Word applies. If you are a woman, they can help you evaluate a potential spouse and provide protection from unsuitable men.[73]

So, benefit from your parents, but move forward from the parent/child relationship which calls you to "obey" them and into a parent/adult relationship which calls you to "honor" them. A child must do both. An adult son or daughter (who is really living like an adult) is simply called to honor his or her mother and father. This transition may be more of a process that unfolds over time rather than a one-time event, but it must happen if you are moving towards marriage.

---

[71] Some younger adults want "to have their cake and eat it too." They want to be treated like an adult when it comes to the freedom to make their own choices, but they want mom and dad to finance their lifestyle.

[72] I say "often" because I realize there may be significant barriers and issues in your relationship with your parents. If this is the case, ask an older godly man or woman in your church to help you work through those issues.

[73] If your parents are not in a position to do this (because of physical or emotional distance) you should rely more heavily on church leadership to help you in this process.

Seek a Spouse with God-Honoring Methods

Let me start out by saying that I do not have "the biblical method for finding a spouse." Sorry to disappoint some of you. The Bible simply does not offer a method. It does *describe* plenty of methods, but I don't think these descriptions are intended to be emulated.

Think for example of the way Adam found Eve. God put him to sleep and formed her from his rib (Gen. 2:21-22). I am pretty sure you should not take this as your plan for finding a mate (you will be waiting forever). Or, think of the method used by the tribe of Benjamin, in the Old Testament. They had a bunch of men and no women to marry them. So, they waited in ambush to kidnap a bunch of single women who were dancing at a festival (Judges 21:16-23). I do not recommended this method (it will land you in prison).

I could go on, but the point is that there is not some biblical command on *how* to find a spouse. All of the methods we could look at in the Bible are descriptive, not prescriptive. The context of each situation makes this clear. The Bible does not promote dating, courting, arranged marriages or any other method.

That being said, it is not as though the Bible has nothing to say on the subject. The Bible may not be a road map for us here, but it is a compass giving us general, guiding principles that we can apply to our cultural ways of doing things. In the West, we primarily use the method of dating. We have already discussed many things which would apply to how we think about relationships in general. Here, however, I want to zoom in on how to apply biblical truth to the question of methods -- specifically, dating. Does the Bible give us any direction when it comes to issues of whom we can date or how to pursue a dating relationship?

A Method to Avoid: Missionary Dating

I have heard it said that the Bible says nothing against a Christian dating a non-believer. Most Christians would at least agree that such a situation is not ideal, but I have seen several men and women, in desperation, enter into such relationships. Usually they begin by saying they will not date the non-Christian, and that they are simply spending *a lot* of time together in order to try and win them to Christ. Before long however they are in a dating relationship, now saying that they would never consider marrying the nonbeliever unless he or she becomes a Christian.

I will not sugar-coat this for you. This is a method which the Bible *requires* you to avoid. Seeking a spouse among unbelievers is not a God-honoring method. I am not saying there is a verse that says, "Thou shalt not date nonbelievers." That does not mean the Bible allows for it. In fact, there are many areas of life the Bible doesn't explicitly address which it, nonetheless, clearly prohibits in principle. For example, it does not say, "You cannot participate in a Ponzi scheme."[74] But there are clear biblical principles that would prohibit it (ex. not lying, not stealing, etc.). In the same way, the culture in which the Bible was written didn't have what we know as dating, but the Bible still has much to say about the issues surrounding modern dating.

---

[74] A Ponzi scheme is offering people an investment opportunity which is really a fraudulent attempt to get their money from them in such a way that they do not notice the theft for a very long time.

The Bible clearly addresses the way Christians are to relate to non-Christians, and it is in a way which prohibits pursuing close relationships (i.e., dating and marriage). I will show you several passages that teach this, but there are many others.

First, in 2 Corinthians 6:14-15 Paul says,

> Do not be unequally yoked with unbelievers. For what partnership has righteousness with lawlessness? Or what fellowship has light with darkness? What accord has Christ with Belial? Or what portion does a believer share with an unbeliever?

In the context, Paul is telling the Corinthians how they are to show their love towards him, the one who is a spiritual father to them (v. 13). There was a faction that was rejecting his apostolic authority, and he is telling the Corinthians not to be yoked with these unbelievers. To be yoked is to be "hitched up" together. The picture is that of two animals hitched together with a yoke to plow a field. So, this is an illustration of the fact that Christians must not be tied together or closely allied with unbelievers. Specifically, in this passage, Paul is saying not to be in close alliance with those who are unbelievers and stirring up division in the church. But the principle would apply to any situation in which Christians would link closely with those who do not serve the same Lord. The reason I say this is that Paul grounds his specific command in the broader principle that those who are seeking the righteousness of God should have no intimate relationship with those who serve false gods (which is every unbeliever).

To make this clearer, Paul goes on in verses 16-18 to say that we (Christians) are the people of God. He is quoting from several Old Testament passages in which the Israelites are called God's people and told to be separate from unbelieving nations around them. Paul is now applying to New Testament believers this idea of being set apart to God. Think about it: in the Old Testament, God was very clear that intermarrying with the pagans was not acceptable. It would lead the Israelites away from God. The same is true today. Those who are closest to us will influence our walk with the Lord.[75]

Since I've found that the pull towards justifying dating or marriage relationships with unbelievers can be strong for singles, I want to look at another passage to bolster my point. In 1 Corinthians 7:39, Paul says, "A wife is bound to her husband as long as he lives. But if her husband dies, she is free to be married to whom she wishes, only in the Lord." Here, Paul is specifically addressing the issue of marriage. Here, he has a word for widowed women who are in the position of picking a spouse. They can choose whomever they want as long as he is "in the Lord" (i.e., a Christian).

In New Testament times, a woman was not likely to be able to choose her first spouse. This was usually arranged by her parents. So, if she was going to choose who to marry, it would have been after being widowed. In such a case, where she gets the choice, she is required to marry a Christian. Therefore, in our culture, in which we have the choice of

---

[75] This does not mean you may divorce a non-believing spouse. Paul explicitly rejects this in 1 Cor. 7:12. But it does mean that before marriage you must make the choice to not enter into such a relationship (cf. 1 Cor. 7:39).

whom we will marry, we must marry a Christian -- end of story.

"But what if I just date them? I won't marry them unless they become a Christian." The Bible still says this is an ungodly relationship. There are three reasons I say this.

The first reason this is ungodly is that it lacks Christian love for others. In chapter 5, I have already elaborated on the idea of dating with no intent on marrying. So, I will just mention that it is unloving because it is basically using the other person so that you can have enjoyment and companionship.

Second, if you are hoping that he or she becomes a Christian so you can get married, I believe you are being confusing and manipulative towards the nonbeliever. This attitude confuses your unbelieving date because you say your ultimate allegiance is to Christ, and then you pursue a degree of intimacy with a person who does not have Jesus as their Lord. It looks as if Jesus' lordship just means you try to live a morally upright life, instead of revealing that He really rules over every area of your life (including your human relationships). This can also be manipulative because it is like dangling the carrot of a deeper relationship in front of your non-believing friend if only they will convert. This all seems to reek of worldly thinking and not Christian love.

Finally, this is an issue of where your ultimate love is focused. I am convinced that the reason most Christians date an unbeliever is that they love and desire a human relationship more than they desire to love Jesus. They may not say that, but their actions seem to prove it. Jesus calls us to a devotion to Himself that allows for no rivals. Even our relationship with a Christian spouse cannot be allowed to overshadow our love for Him. Jesus said it this way, in Matthew 10:37-39,

> Whoever loves father or mother more than me is not worthy of me, and whoever loves son or daughter more than me is not worthy of me. And whoever does not take his cross and follow me is not worthy of me. Whoever finds his life will lose it, and whoever loses his life for my sake will find it.

This is a sobering thought. Am I willing to die to self to really live in Christ? If the answer is "No," then we do not have the life of Christ in us. If the answer is "Yes," then every other relationship is properly ordered *under* our allegiance to Jesus and His will. Believing the lie that satisfaction is found ultimately in human relationships rather than our relationship to Christ is deadly to the soul.

The great bishop from the 1800's, JC Ryle, advised young men to "never make an intimate friend of anyone who is not a friend of God." This is a long quote, but worth a close reading. He said,

> Believe me, the importance of this advice cannot be overrated. There is no telling the harm that is done by associating with godless companions and friends. The devil has few better helps in ruining a man's soul. Grant him this help, and he cares little for all the armor with which you may be armed against him. Good education, early habits of morality, sermons, books, regular homes, letters of parents—all, he knows well, will avail you little if you cling to ungodly friends. You may resist many open temptations, refuse many plain snares; but once take up a bad companion, and he is content. ... You must recollect,

we are all creatures of imitation: precept may teach us, but it is example that draws us. There is that in us all, that we are always disposed to catch the ways of those with whom we live; and the more we like them, the stronger does the disposition grow. Without our being aware of it, they influence our tastes and opinions; we gradually give up what they dislike and take up what they like, in order to become more close friends with them. And worst of all, we catch their ways in things that are wrong far quicker than in things that are right. Health, unhappily, is not contagious, but disease is. It is far more easy [sic] to catch a chill than to impart a glow; and to make each other's religion dwindle away, than grow and prosper. Young men, I ask you to lay these things to heart. Before you let anyone become your constant companion, before you get into the habit of telling him everything, and going to him in all your troubles and all your pleasures—before you do this, just think of what I have been saying, Ask yourself, "Will this be a useful friendship to me or not?" [76]

Please don't misunderstand. Ryle's point, and mine, is not that you must avoid unbelievers like the plague. We must love and reach out to unbelievers. We do not fear becoming "unclean" merely by relating to unbelievers.

The point is, will this friendship help you better love God? If so, then a close friendship is permitted. If it will not, then your relationship with them is not that of a close friendship. If you don't have Christ in common, then you are, by definition, going in two very different directions despite any

---

[76] *Thoughts for Young Men* (Pensecola, FL: Chapel Library, 2006), PDF accessed from www.chapellibrary.org, pg. 27.

"chemistry" you might feel or common interests you may have. You serve God, and they are under the power of Satan (John 8:44, 2 Cor. 4:4). You are in the Kingdom of God, and they are in the domain of darkness (Col. 1:13). Therefore, your relationship to an unbeliever is one of seeking to rescue them from a burning building, not of slow dancing with them by the light of the fire of coming judgment.

Dear brother or sister, perhaps you are in an "unequally yoked" relationship. Maybe you have never given much thought to what the Bible says on this issue. Perhaps you have not given much thought to your own motives in dating a nonbeliever. I urge you to consider the passages mentioned above and to examine your own motives. If you are already in a relationship with a nonbeliever, you must end it. Do it graciously and humbly (admitting how you have sinned against the Lord and them), but do it you must. Ask an older godly man or woman in your church to help you think about how to do this in a way that shows love to the other person and which upholds your undivided devotion to your Lord.

A Method to be Cautious of: Online Dating

In God's providence, you and I live in a time of amazing technological advancements. Through the internet, we have the ability to communicate with people whom we might otherwise have not met. This has given rise to online dating sites.

I do not think the Bible prohibits online dating by direct command or by indirect principles. But I do think there are some biblical principles which we must take into account. *Below are six cautions to take into consideration.*

The first is the issue of motivation. In one sense this is not unique to online dating. As Christians, we realize that God cares about our motives, and, so, we must always seek to have God-honoring motives. When it comes to online dating, it would be good to consider why you are doing this. Is it out of desperation? Is it motivated by doubting that God is able (or willing) to bring you a spouse? Is it an attempt to force a relationship to happen on *your* time table? It might be or it might not. Perhaps you are content with where the Lord has you and see this as a means by which you are responsibly pursuing marriage.

The second issue to be cautious about regarding this form of finding a date is the lack of "natural" interactions. When you meet someone at church, work, or school, you typically have the opportunity to naturally get to know him or her over time. You can observe their character and interact with them as friends before initiating a dating relationship. Online dating, however, generally means that the first time you communicate is with the explicit intention of finding a date/mate. You may not have opportunities to simply observe them in group settings and to allow the relationship to naturally develop.

The third issue is a potential lack of accountability. Online dating allows you to have interactions with a member of the opposite sex without your church community knowing the details. It has the potential to encourage isolation as well, since you probably do not have common circles of friends. Isolation is dangerous because sin and temptation abound in such conditions. Sin is deceitful, especially when we are isolated (see Heb. 3:12-13).

The fourth issue is that online dating makes it easier for you to misrepresent your qualities and downplay your shortcomings (they can do the same thing). I once saw a commercial in which a young woman is telling her neighbor that anything you read on the internet is true. She then says she is waiting for her date, a French model she met online, to show up. Just then an overweight, unattractive American man wearing a fanny pack walks up and says "Bonjour." Without flinching she walks down the street with her "model" date. You can't believe everything you read online, and a lack of community and face to face interactions makes it easier to be deceived and to deceive.

The fifth issue is that online dating may promote laziness and lack of courage in men. Let's face it, finding a date requires courage. Asking a woman out means the risk of being shot down. And it takes a lot more risk to spend time serving and getting to know the single women in your church than it does to sit in front of your computer with your PJ's on and scroll through a bunch of profiles on the screen.

Finally, online dating tends to more easily promote self-seeking relationships. Again, every relationship could be this way. But in online dating, you are looking at a bunch of people and evaluating their qualities to decide if you want to "buy in" to a date. It can become consumeristic, instead of a servant-oriented way of thinking about others. The temptation is to treat the people as profiles: to treat the person as if they were a piece of furniture on the Antique Roadshow to be evaluated to determine their real worth. This is not necessarily true, but the potential for this must be carefully guarded against.

If you plan on being involved with online dating (or already are), let me offer a few pieces of wisdom to help you avoid these potential pitfalls.

The first thing is to involve an older, godly Christian brother or sister who has a solid perspective on biblical relationships and who will hold you accountable. Give them access to your profile and messages. This will allow them to keep you honest and to keep your communication wholesome and God-honoring. It is also important to have their help in protecting you from harm since online dating may lend itself to predators.

The next thing I would suggest is to limit your search to singles in a radius that is within easy driving distance. If the potential date is too far away, you run the risk of being in an isolated relationship and lack the opportunity to get to see each other interact in groups of peers (a good place to see the person's character). You also run the risk of being a poor steward of the time and money God has given you if you begin a relationship which requires long trips to see each other.

Third, make sure you talk theology with any potential date. You don't have to grill your new friend (especially not on the first date). But, you need to find out what they believe about important doctrines such as who God is, how to be rightly related to God, the authority of the Bible, etc. Theology is extremely important because it affects the way you live out your faith. Since you are not meeting in the same church, you need to spend a little more time checking to make sure you have agreement on major biblical issues.

Fourth, take the relationship offline and into the church community as quickly as you can. Spend time getting to know each other in groups of friends. You probably shouldn't immediately start attending their church,[77] but you should involve people from your church and their church in the process as much as possible.

Conclusion

We have spent a lot of time looking at an approach to dating that should be avoided and another of which you should be cautious. You may be wondering, "What approach should I employ in seeking a spouse?" While the Bible doesn't give us a particular method, it does give us some direction. In the next chapter, I will spend some time on this subject.

---

[77] I say this because this may move the level of commitment up too quickly. Switching churches is a big deal. You have made a commitment to your local body of believers. You should not leave those relationships lightly. Obviously, if you are engaged or married, you should be worshiping and serving side by side in the same church with your fiancé or spouse.

9

Finding a Good Thing:

Biblical principles for finding a spouse

Don't you wish that you had it as easy as Adam and Eve? I mean, it was pretty obvious who they would marry. It was so uncomplicated. There was no wondering, "Is she the one?" It is more complicated for us. For starters, we have to contend with our sinful desires and motives and those of others. In addition, we have many more "options." That actually seems to make things more difficult. A plethora of possible mates can paralyze us because we have anxiety over missing out.

I understand these feelings, but I think we often tend to overcomplicate things. In order to be "marriage material," the other person really only needs to be a Christian (not just in name, but in reality) and eligible for marriage (i.e., not already married, not unbiblically divorced, and a member of the opposite sex).

That being said, since we do not live in a culture in which we simply line up all the eligible Christian men on one side of the fellowship hall and all the Christian ladies on the other side and then pair them off for marriage, we must think about how to go about pursuing a spouse. Proverbs says "He who finds a wife finds a good thing" (18:22). So, how do you find a good thing?

Pray

I believe prayer is one of the most neglected and abused means of grace. It is easy to abuse prayer by turning it into a magic rabbit's foot or a bell we ring to get God to come be our cosmic butler. On the other hand, it is often neglected because we assume that prayer really doesn't do anything. "If God has a sovereign plan, then why should I pray?" the reasoning goes.

There are several reasons we must pray. First, we have a relationship with the *living* God who is our Father (Matt. 6:9). He is not some force. He cares for us and calls us to relate to Him in prayer (Matt. 7:8-11). Second, God commands us to pray (1 Thess. 5:17). Third, prayer is the means through which God does His sovereign work. God is sovereign over the outcomes *and* the way in which He accomplishes those outcomes. God sovereignly causes us to pray and uses those prayers in accomplishing exactly what He intends to do.

Therefore, we should pray, and that includes praying for a godly spouse. We should pray with faith that God can provide what we are requesting and that He delights to give good gifts to His children (Matt. 7:8-11). We should pray that

God is at work in us, conforming us to the image of Christ. We should pray that He would help us to examine our own heart and motives in our pursuit of a spouse. We should ask Him to give us wisdom in deciding how to best order our relationships so that we faithfully love and serve those He has placed around us. And we should ask Him to give us a spouse that will help us glorify Him.

This does not mean He will give us a spouse when we want one. It does not mean He must give us a spouse at all. So, pray for God to give you the blessing of a spouse while trusting Him with your desires.

Do not skip over this. And don't see it merely as step one in finding a mate. Prayer is like breathing for the Christian. There may be times of more intense prayer because we are in circumstances that make us feel out of breath. There are times where prayer is more routine. But there is never a time when it stops unless you are dead (and then you shall see Him face to face).

Examine God's Providence, But Don't Try to Read It

Sometimes when we think about praying for a spouse we quickly begin to pray for God to reveal His sovereign will to us. In other words, we ask God to show us what the future holds. It isn't wrong to ask God to sovereignly direct your steps (Prov. 3:5-6). But, when we get fixated on figuring out His hidden, future will, we tend to overcomplicate things and set ourselves up for trouble.

When looking for a spouse, we should examine God's providential[78] dealings. The situations He places you in do affect your pursuit of a spouse. Are you in major debt, still finishing school, or about to move to a new place for work? All these things will affect your decisions about when and how you will pursue a dating relationship. In addition, as a finite being, you cannot meet every eligible Christian on the planet. So, you must take into account God's providence by considering those He has placed in your life.

However, we should not look at situations as "signs" from God. We often get into trouble because we start trying to interpret God's *hidden* will for our lives by reading His providential dealings. The problem is that we cannot know God's sovereign will for us outside of what He has clearly told us in His Word (ex. Christ is returning for us, we will be with Him in heaven, and other prophecies in the Bible). But we often start to try and figure out the future by looking at what God is doing. We don't like having to walk by faith, so we begin looking at circumstances as another channel of special revelation from God.

Don't assume that just because this is the first guy to take an interest in you since you started praying for a spouse that he is "the one." He might be, but he might not be. Just because she likes to watch science fiction movies does not mean that God is telling you to marry her.

You can take all those things as God's providential dealings, but you must not pretend like they are secret communications from God that you must decode. *God doesn't call you to*

---

[78] By providential I simply mean God's sovereign, hidden will as we see it being played out in our lives.

interpret His providence. God calls you to humbly live under His providence. He expects you to trust Him by applying His Word, found in the Bible, to everyday decisions.

Faithfully Tend to Your God-Given Responsibilities

Instead of wasting time trying to develop methods for decoding secret messages from God, you should focus on faithfully fulfilling your God-given responsibilities. What responsibilities do you have right now?

To help you determine your God-given responsibilities you should consider your God-given roles. You are a church member (at least I hope you are). That comes with certain responsibilities to serve and minister to others in the body of Christ. Perhaps you are a student or have a job. God gives you the responsibility of serving your employer or of learning for the sake of blessing others down the road. If you are still dependent on your parents then you have responsibilities to obey them.

My point is that you should not think that your only responsibility is to find a spouse (assuming you desire marriage). You have other God-given roles that you must fulfill. You should not be unfaithful to what God has given you to do. So, as you look for a spouse, keep living the normal Christian life in all the areas God has placed you, and enjoy doing it.

Initiating a Relationship

While you are praying and living out your Christian life, God may bring along a man or woman that you are interested in getting to know a little better. There are a few things I would counsel you to do.

Evaluate What Attracts You to This Person

Are you *just* attracted to his or her physical appearance? Physical appearance is not the main thing when it comes to marriage. God is more concerned with the heart (1 Pet. 3:4; 1 Sam. 16:7). You should have the same concern, because what pleases God should please you. Also, be wise enough to realize that physical beauty fades in this fallen world.

The Bible does not place an emphasis on outward appearances, though it does acknowledge that there is such a thing as beauty and attraction. Our culture, however, seems to be all bent out of shape over this issue. We, too easily, elevate beauty and issues of attraction higher than what God says is important (i.e., godly character). We quickly become worldly or self-focused and put the emphasis on our tastes and preferences. Men, we do a disservice to our Christian sisters when we talk about how attractive godly character is and then fawn over ungodly, outwardly attractive women or when we refuse to consider a godly woman just because she is not what we envisioned our wife looking like (the same goes for you, ladies). God's Word also tells us we are being foolish: "Charm is deceitful, and beauty is vain, but a woman who fears the Lord is to be praised" (Prov. 31:30).

So, are you attracted to this person for the right reasons? Do you see a godliness and love for God's Word and God's people in this person?

Make a Move, Man!

Yes, you! You have the responsibility to exercise leadership and to take the bulk of the risk in a relationship. This is a practical way to protect her and to show biblical masculinity. The way you should do this is to approach her about it. Do not be like a second grader who tries to do reconnaissance by asking her friends how she feels about you. And do not be manipulative by saying God told you to ask her out. If she is smart, she will say she didn't get the memo from God on that one.

Some of you men are wondering if you should talk to her dad. I would say maybe. If her dad would appreciate it, then you should be willing to approach him. If he goes to the same church as you, then I would strongly recommend that you approach him. But, if she is older and has been living independently for a long time or if her dad is distant in his relationship with her, you may not need to talk to him first. However, it may be good to talk to her pastor or some other man who is seeking to protect her. The biblical principle is to protect her and to honor any God-given authorities in her life. There is no command to ask her dad, but in many circumstances it may be a very good way to apply the biblical principles of love and honor.

Respond to His Initiative, Woman

Women, if you see a man you are interested in, then you should continue to serve and love others while trying to observe his character and conduct. Do not take the role of initiating and leading this relationship. That is not the way a godly marriage functions, and it should not characterize a relationship you are hoping will lead to marriage. If he begins sending mixed signals about his intentions, by singling you out and not officially trying to begin a relationship, you might need to ask him to clarify his desire. Your job is to be ready to respond to his leadership. I know this may seem counter to your desire to "make things happen," but it is a good opportunity to trust God to accomplish His will in your life. Don't manipulate the situation. Trust God.

If you are not interested in him, then tell him. And don't blame it on God. Don't say, "The Holy Spirit is telling me we shouldn't date." He can handle being rejected by you, but not the Holy Spirit. He shows love by taking the risk and you show love by being clear and kind in your response.

Evaluating the Relationship

If a relationship begins, you should be sure you are evaluating it from a biblical perspective. [79] Just because it "feels right" doesn't mean it is a good relationship. And just because each of you has flaws doesn't mean you should end a relationship (if that were the case, only Jesus would be qualified to be your date).

This is a key aspect of pursuing marriage. JC Ryle points us to why it is important when he wrote,

> And who can estimate the importance of a right choice in marriage? It is a step which, according to the old saying, "either makes a man or mars him." Your happiness in

---

[79] To help in evaluating a relationship I suggest using the article "Should We Get Married? Five 'Pre engagement' Questions to Ask Yourselves," by David Powlison and John Yenchko. You can purchase it at www.ccef.org.

both lives may depend on it. Your wife must either help your soul or harm it: there is no medium. She will either fan the flame of religion in your heart, or throw cold water upon it and make it burn low. She will either be wings or fetters, a rein or a spur to your Christianity, according to her character. He that findeth a good wife doth indeed "findeth a good thing" (Pro 18:22).[80]

You should evaluate whether or not the relationship encourages each of you to love, obey, and serve God. Do you encourage each other to know God's Word and to obey it? Is he demonstrating qualities that indicate he is a good spiritual leader?[81] Is she supportive of godly leadership? Is Christ central to each of you and to your relationship? You are not just looking for someone who *says* they love Jesus. You are looking for someone who *demonstrates* a genuine love for Jesus in obedience to Him (John 14:21).

You should also consider whether or not the relationship is helping you love and serve others or if it is becoming inward focused. God calls you to serve and love others in the body of Christ, not just a particular person you are interested in pursuing for the purpose of marriage.

Another area to examine is your track record of handling conflict. When you get two sinful people together there will be times of conflict. When those times come, how do you handle it? Do work through them in a God-honoring way?

---

[80] *Thoughts for Young Men* (Pensecola, FL: Chapel Library, 2006), PDF accessed from www.chapellibrary.org, pg. 28.

[81] He doesn't have to be a more intelligent than you to be able to do this. He just needs to love God even more than he loves you.

Being willing to solve problems in a biblical way is key to a God-honoring relationship.

As things progress, you should look to see if you are heading in the same direction in life. If his desire is to be a Bible translator in Papua New Guinea and your desire is to live in Tallahassee, Florida and serve in your local church, then you need to have some serious discussion about that difference. If you marry one another, you will need to be going in one direction. Once you are married you are on the same path whether you like it or not. So, take time to evaluate it now. Obviously, you do not know what the future holds, but you must plan your ways even as you trust the Lord to direct your steps (Prov. 3:5-6).

As I have mentioned before, make sure to include an older godly man and woman in the process. Ask them to help evaluate your relationship. It is easy to let ourselves be blinded by infatuation. A godly Christian friend can often see these blind spots and help us see where we are ignoring problems or where we are making a bigger issue out of something than we really should.

If at any time it becomes clear that this relationship does not need to continue, you should lovingly let the other person know. It is not kind to let things continue once you have decided not to pursue marriage to this person.

That brings us to our last point. How do you proceed when things are going well?

Moving towards Marriage

If the relationship is progressing in a healthy, God-honoring way, then you should be moving towards the goal of marriage. Don't drag things on needlessly. Make a commitment.

You may be fearful of committing. You might wonder if a better person may come along. Let me challenge you to evaluate your thinking. Are you being self-centered in this thought? If this person is a godly man or woman who is your friend and cares about your well-being, what else do you need? Our culture has given us the idea that we must find "the one." The idea is that there is one person with whom we will experience some amazing chemistry. But, when you look to Scripture you see nothing about "the one" or about "chemistry." You simply see Christians loving and serving one another.

Don't misunderstand. I am not saying you should move into engagement and marriage if there are major red flags in the relationship. Major sin patterns and ungodliness will not change with marriage. Additionally, I am not saying you must marry someone you do not want to marry. You should have a desire to be a husband or wife *to this individual.* Deal with major issues, but if there are not any, and you desire to marry this person, then move towards marriage.

Men, this is again the place for you to exercise leadership. Don't wait for writing in the sky or some sign from God. Ask others who know you and her well to help you evaluate things. If they do not have any biblical reasons for you to put off marriage, then move forward. Ask her to marry you and if she says, "Yes!," then pursue premarital counseling from your pastor.

You may wonder why you should do premarital counseling. I could give you a lot of good reasons, but let me just give you an analogy. Many people spend four years of their life in college preparing for their job. If we spend that much time preparing for a job, how much more should we be willing to invest in preparing for marriage? I am not advocating four years of preparation. I am saying you should meet with your pastor or a godly man and his wife to learn what God's Word says about the challenges you will face in marriage.

Conclusion

Pursuing marriage is not easy. There is not a biblical list of 10 steps to finding a spouse. Though things are more complicated than they were for Adam and Eve, we have God's sure Word to direct us in our pursuit of marriage. In this chapter, I have outlined a way of applying some of these biblical principles to the area of seeking a spouse. May God give you wisdom and love to handle all your relationships in a way which demonstrates a love for God and neighbor.

Conclusion:

A Wedding Reception That Will Change Our Lives

As a man, my perspective on wedding receptions is that they serve one main purpose: they provide food of some sort. I suppose I should be more biblical and affirm that receptions provide a chance for the community of God to celebrate the nuptials they just witnessed with the newly married couple. Even with these good purposes, most of us would agree that we have never been to a wedding reception that changed our life. But the truth is, if you are a Christian, there is a wedding reception which will fill your heart with such joy that you will feel as if your heart is about to explode out of your chest. Before we get to that, let's watch Jesus demolish our shortsighted view of marriage that stops us from seeing the wonders of what is to come.

Human Marriage is a Picture of Something Greater

A group of Sadducees approached Jesus and the spokesman of the group stepped forward. You can almost see the glimmer in his eye as he put Jesus to the test. The group thought they had Him right where they wanted Him. This little think tank devised a scenario that they thought would prove that Jesus was not the Messiah and that there is no such thing as the resurrection from the dead. Rubbing his fingers through his beard, the spokesman confidently began his "question."

> "Teacher, Moses wrote for us that if a man's brother dies and leaves a wife, but leaves no child, the man must take the widow and raise up offspring for his brother. There were seven brothers; the first took a wife, and when he died left no offspring. And the second took her, and died, leaving no offspring. And the third likewise. And the seven left no offspring. Last of all the woman also died. *In the resurrection, when they rise again, whose wife will she be? For the seven had her as wife"* (Mark 12:19-23).

I imagine that the group let out a collective chuckle and waited for what they thought would be Jesus hem hawing to buy time. But, what they got was quick and firm rebuke.

> Jesus said to them, "Is this not the reason you are wrong, because you know neither the Scriptures nor the power of God? *For when they rise from the dead, they neither marry nor are given in marriage,* but are like angels in heaven" (Mark 12:24-25, emphasis added).

There were two problems with the Sadducees' presuppositions, and Jesus drops bunker-busting bombs on them both. First, they did not know the Scriptures. God's Word clearly teaches that there is a resurrection. Second, they did not know the power of God. That is, they did not believe that God had the power to raise people from the dead and make the eternal state of their existence much more wonderful than the current one. They assumed this world was all there was. They were so caught up in the present that they refused to see the glorious realities of the resurrection.

They assumed that they could disprove the resurrection (and need for a Savior) by showing how crazy an eternal state would be. It would be ludicrous to try and sort out the woman's relationship to these seven men if there was a resurrection. She would be polyandrous. *Their critical error, however, was failing to see that marriage is a temporary reality pointing to an eternal reality.* You see, no one is married in heaven because the shadow of human marriage will give way to the realities of heaven. That reality is the relationship between Jesus and His bride, the Church.

Don't assume this means marriage in this life is unimportant to God's eternal purposes. On the contrary, it was designed by God to testify to the reality and beauty of Jesus' relationship to His Church. Ephesians 5:31-32 says,

> "Therefore a man shall leave his father and mother and hold fast to his wife, and the two shall become one flesh." This mystery is profound, and I am saying that it refers to Christ and the church.

Men, if you marry, realize that the way you love, lead, provide for, and protect your wife has everything to do with picturing Jesus' covenant with His Church. Women, if you marry, realize that the way you affirm and respond to your husband's leadership puts the Church's relationship with Christ on display.

But what does this mean for those who remain single their whole life? John Piper writes,

> This has profound significance for singleness in this life. It means that if two wives will not be one too many [referring to those who remarry after the death of a spouse], then no wives will not be one too few. If love in the age to come is transposed into a key above and beyond the melody of marriage in this life, then singleness here will prove to be no disadvantage in eternity.[82]

I hope that you see that it is no disadvantage to be single *now,* either. Your singleness, just like marriage, serves to point to the eternal realities of the gospel message. How so?

For those who remain *single by choice,* you testify to the world that being part of Jesus' family matters more than physical ties and offspring. Our world's motto is, "You only live once." And the perspective has been pervasive throughout the history of fallen mankind. But when you choose to live in a way that shows having spiritual offspring and contentment in your heavenly family is all you need, then you stand as a beacon of light for eternal realities.

For those who are *single by trial* and yet demonstrate contentment in the Lord, you too testify to the gospel. You bear witness that God is good and that your inheritance is not of this world. You prove that your own desires do not rule you, but Christ does. You demonstrate faith in God to a world which believes in only what it sees. When you seek to have spiritual offspring, even while your desire for physical offspring is unmet, you show that the family of God is more

---

[82] "For Single Men and Women," in *Recovering Biblical Manhood and Womanhood,* Ed. John Piper & Wayne Grudem (Wheaton, IL: Crossway Books, 2006), pg. 13.

important than physical life. When you walk humbly with your Savior, even when you do not have an earthly spouse, you show that Jesus is your all.

The Banquet Hall of Heaven

As I said at the beginning of this chapter, there is coming a wedding banquet which will fill you with unspeakable joy. Marriage and singleness both point to it, and the married and single, rejoice when it comes. Here is the Apostle John's description of it:

> Then I heard what seemed to be the voice of a great multitude, like the roar of many waters and like the sound of mighty peals of thunder, crying out,
>
> > "Hallelujah!
> > For the Lord our God
> >   the Almighty reigns.
> > Let us rejoice and exult
> >   and give him the glory,
> > for the marriage of the Lamb has come,
> >   and his Bride has made herself ready;
> > it was granted her to clothe herself
> >   with fine linen, bright and pure" —
>
> for the fine linen is the righteous deeds of the saints.
>
> And the angel said to me, "Write this: Blessed are those who are invited to the marriage supper of the Lamb." And he said to me, "These are the true words of God" (Revelation 19:7-9).

This is your wedding reception, Christian! True blessing, everlasting happiness, belongs to "those who are invited to the marriage supper of the Lamb." At this table will be gathered all Christians. At this supper, none of them will be married to each other, because they are all, together, married to Jesus Christ.

This is not some weird "Jesus is my boyfriend" type of thing. This is the glorious reality to which human marriage points. It is the fullness of the reality that we, God's people, are one with our Savior. We belong to Him. His love, protection, and joy belong to us. Our allegiance belongs to Him, and our everlasting happiness is found in Him.

The Final Word

Your eternal state begins with our collective feasting at the marriage supper of the Lamb. We have covered many practical matters, which are important in this life. But do not lose sight of the purpose of marriage and singleness. He who finds a wife finds a good thing. The one who is seated at the marriage supper of the Lamb lacks no good thing. Now that is a wedding reception I look forward to attending.

Made in the USA
San Bernardino, CA
07 June 2018